Codependency No More

How to Cure Codependency, Start to Love Yourself and Fight for No More Codependent Relationship Ever

Author:
Elisabeth Cloud

Furthermore, the information that can be found within the pages described forthwith shall be considered both accurate and truthful when it comes to the recounting of facts. As such, any use, correct or incorrect, of the provided information will render the Publisher free of responsibility as to the actions taken outside of their direct purview. Regardless, there are zero scenarios where the original author or the Publisher can be deemed liable in any fashion for any damages or hardships that may result from any of the information discussed herein.

Additionally, the information in the following pages is intended only for informational purposes and should thus be thought of as universal. As befitting its nature, it is presented without assurance regarding its prolonged validity or interim quality. Trademarks that are mentioned are done without written consent and can in no way be considered an endorsement from the trademark holder.

Table Of Contents

Introduction

Congratulations on purchasing *Codependency No More: How to Cure Codependency, Start to Love Yourself and Fight for No More Codependent Relationship Ever*, and thank you for doing so.

The following chapters will discuss everything about codependency and so if you are wondering whether you are codependent or not and how you can overcome it, then this book is just the right one for you. There are different degrees of being codependent, and there are so many people who are in a codependent relationship, and it is much more than you thought. Also, you should not relate being codependent to being unhappy, but it is also true that some of them are in pain.

It is often noticed that codependents are mostly attracted to codependents, and that is why they end up having unhealthy relationships. But with proper commitment and support, you can reverse the codependent symptoms. If you do not check your codependent behavior at the right time, it can easily affect your thinking abilities. Well, you shouldn't think of codependency as something that you can get rid of overnight either because it doesn't happen that way. You have to work yourself up to your goal. But once you take your first step towards recovery, you will start to see the world in a whole new light.

There are plenty of books on this subject on the market, thanks again for choosing this one! Every effort was made to ensure it is full of as much useful information as possible. Please enjoy!

Chapter 1:

What Is Codependency?

I am assuming that you are totally new to the concept of codependency, and so, in this first chapter, I want to give you an overview of the concept. Every relationship has its ups and downs. There are times when you will feel that you are so much in love, and there will also be times when that other person will disappoint you or hurt you. Just like the addictive behavior shown by addicts towards drugs, codependents have a similar kind of thing in relationships. The life of a codependent person is always around someone else, that is, the person or people they love. They do not know how to live for themselves, and their thoughts are always preoccupied with the people they love.

Definition of Codependency

There is no formal definition of codependency even today. It is still a highly debated topic of discussion around the world. However, a tentative definition of the term was coined in the year 1989 in a national conference by 22 leaders who stated that codependency is a type of painful dependence and it involved a typical behavior involving approval by others and compulsive behaviors all of which is done to seek self-worth, safety, and identity.

Is Codependency an Addiction?

In 1988, Timmen Cermak, a psychiatrist, said that codependency should be called a disease. Yes, called it a disease does sound a bit morbid, but what he meant to say was that codependency is a condition displaying progressive symptoms and that it can heavily impact the normal functioning of a person.

But, some people are strictly against the label of the disease being put on codependency. This is because they think it discourages, stigmatizes, and also causes a disempowerment of the person who is actually trying to tread on the path of recovery. These people claim that labeling it as a disease would only make the people think that they do not really have any control over the problem, and thus, there is no chance of them getting well. But others are not aligned with this view. Instead, they think that the punitive treatment and shame that comes hand-in-hand with addiction is eliminated by called codependency a disease. These people are of the mentality that addition should be considered as a form of physical disease and treated with empathy.

So, whether you consider codependency to be a disease or an addiction is entirely your decision, but you should know that recovery is possible irrespective of what you consider it to be.

Why is the Percentage of Codependents Mostly Women?

It has been found that women comprise a greater part of the codependent percentage of people than men and it is mostly due to these reasons:

- **Biological**—Women tend to crave relationships as if they are wired for them. They also have a superb ability to bond easily with others, and they also have a much higher level of sensitivity to feelings. You will see that when faced with stress, men often prepare for some kind of action whereas women, on the other hand, will befriend others.

- **Developmental**—It is also seen that while growing up as kids, girls have a more dependable nature on their parents, and they also share a greater amount of emotional involvement. Losing someone or a dent in a relationship is what they fear the most right from their childhood years. They have a greater acceptance of parental values in their lives, and this arises from their very nature. They also tend to show anxiety symptoms whenever their emotional attachment to their parents is threatened due to separation. Thus, one of the biggest challenges that they face in life is autonomy. But boys learn to develop their male identities by separating from their parents. Their biggest challenge is intimacy.

- **Political**—Over the decades and centuries, women have always been subjected to oppression. They have been marginalized and deprived of equal access to rights, money, and power. Women have been traumatized for generations because of sexual and physical abuse. Men have faced it too, but women have faced it in a far greater magnitude. This has lowered their self-esteem to extreme lows.

- **Religion**—Women are often considered to play a subservient role in society and especially to men. This is because of the widespread presence of patriarchy in almost all cultures. Women are often subjected to a condition where they have to defer to their male companions or guardians. They also have less freedom in all aspects of life and also receive a lesser amount of education.

- **Cultural**—You will find that girls are subjected to a greater level of restriction in most cultures around the world, and they do not enjoy that many opportunities for autonomy. Societal norms, along with hormonal changes, encourage the boys to be autonomous and rebellious. Thus, they receive much more freedom.

- **Societal**—Women always show more tendency towards having higher rates of depression and lower self-esteem. I am not saying that this is somehow related to codependency, but it is definitely dependent on how society treats a woman. A study that was conducted by Dove stated that 40% of the total women are not happy with how they look. Society has always set unrealistic standards for women with airbrushed models on the front pages of magazines. And all of this starts in the childhood years where some girls even show self-destructive behavior.

What Codependency Isn't?

If you truly want to understand what codependency is, then you also need to know about all those things which it isn't. It is very common for people to confuse this term with interdependency or caregiving. But it is nothing even remotely close to that.

Caregiving Isn't Codependency

People, and women, in particular, tend to nurture others, including kids, and take care of them. The best example is that of a mother who does everything she can for her kid. But you should not confuse this caregiving nature with codependent caretaking. This is mostly because, in the case of codependence, the percentage of taking is much more than giving. Caretaking is something that arises out of deprivation and need, but caregiving is out of abundance.

This example should make it clearer to you. Suppose you leave your job to take care of your spouse, who is severely ill. But you did not leave your job because you wanted to spend more time with your spouse and that you thought that was your priority. You left it out of guilt that you were not able to be there for your spouse when you should. You can take over everything related to your spouse's treatment, but you do not ask for help from anyone even though you know that you need it. Then after a few days, you start feeling overwhelmed, and you are too worried even though your spouse may not be needing you as much you claim. You do not take care of your own needs, and you feel bad about that too, and you are tired all the time. All of this is an example where you are codependent on your spouse.

Codependency Doesn't Mean Being Kind

It is natural for a person to be kind to someone else or help them out. But it is low self-esteem that gives way to codependent pleasing, which, in turn, is not an act of kindness. Codependent people don't have a choice because their mindset is such that they cannot say no to anything. They do not help out others because they want to. Rather, they help out others from a state of fear, guilt, or insecurity.

For example, if you usually order takeout or eat at budget restaurants, but when it comes to your girlfriend, you let her choose the pricey ones because of shame, then this is being codependent. You are letting shame take over you as to what will your girlfriend think of you. This is not kindness. You are not taking her to a pricey restaurant as some sort of grand gesture. You are doing it to maintain a higher self-image. Also, if you are taking your girlfriend to a luxury place because you think otherwise, she might leave, then it is a case of bribery, and you are codependent on her. If you had asked her to choose any place she likes just because you don't care that much as to where you eat, then it would not have been a case of codependency.

Codependency Is Not Interdependency

A couple who is codependent on each other always faces power struggles, although everything might seem normal from outside. One of the partners might feel guilt after anticipating what the other person needs. For every mood or feeling they have, they get affected and react. To ensure that all their needs are met, they have this habit of always trying to be in control. They fear not only separation but also intimacy because it threatens their insecure selves.

Chapter 2:

Signs That You Are in A Codependent Relationship

E veryone has some inner conflicts or wounds that bring back a surge of feelings that they do not want to face. Are you afraid that people might judge you for what you did or for who you are? Are you afraid that you might get hurt if you love someone or that you might end up alone? These are some wounds that lead to the development of a codependent nature, and you might not even realize when or how all of this will happen. In this chapter, I am going to introduce you to the symptoms of codependency. You might not be having all of these symptoms, but some. But it is important to identify whether you are in a codependent relationship or not.

Internalized Shame

There are a lot of feelings and emotions that come along with shame, and they are inadequacy, unworthiness, and alienation. You might always have this nagging feeling that others can see your flaws, and so you are alienated or exposed. You might simply want to go to one corner and become invisible. But it is not always about your self-esteem because even people with high self-esteem experience shame. Everyone feels shame at some point or the other in their life. If that feeling of shame is stopping you from pursuing something socially unacceptable, then it is a healthy shame, for example, urinating in public.

Shame has a lot of physical signs, as well. Some of them include withdrawing, avoidance of any type of eye contact, perspiring, freezing, nausea, dizziness, and so on. It is usually seen that after a person encounters an incident of embarrassment, the shame passes away. But in the case of someone who is codependent, it is since their childhood years that this shame is internalized. Even if the particular event has been long gone, the shame persists and gets triggered from time to time. It acts like an open wound that doesn't tend to heal. They become ashamed of their own personality, and this feeling frames them as a person.

There will be an intensification of ordinary shame with chronic internalized shame. This kind of shame gives way to anxiety and lasts way longer than others. This also leads to feelings of despair and hopelessness in the codependent individual. Their self-esteem suffers a hit, and they start showing symptoms of codependency like depression, people-pleasing, addiction, and so on. A sense of inferiority also settles in the subconscious mind of the person the moment they start internalizing their shame. They see everything in a negative light and even start comparing themselves to others and especially with those they admire. This can even lead to envy and jealousy. If the jealousy drives them towards positive goal setting without developing any hard feelings for the other person, then that jealousy is good. If the jealousy is making you so much insecure that you have become adamant about taking some harsh steps, then it is bad.

But in most cases, codependent people think that they are not enough, and they are somewhat inferior to the people they admire. This kind of jealousy results in a painful shame. Sometimes, when people are unconscious of the shame that is present inside of them, they start boasting of indulging in too much self-importance, especially in front of them who they supervise. They start devaluing others, and in that phase, they think that they have attained a higher level than the others present around them. The maximum percentage of codependents I have met show a fluctuating character between feeling superior and inferior.

Your self-image is directly affected by internalized shame. The worst part about this kind of shame is that it is not always visible and can silently hide in your unconscious mind. When things go out of control, it can lead you to a spiral of anxiety and depression. Sometimes, the internalized shame is gained from parents in the childhood years where the parents transfer their shame onto the child either through nonverbal behavior or verbal messages.

Lower Levels of Self-Esteem

Self-esteem is different from shame. The former is all about how you see yourself, whereas the latter is merely a feeling. With self-esteem, your actual opinion of yourself comes to light. Depending on how you think of yourself, your self-esteem can either be low or high. But you need to get one thing clear, and that is, self-esteem is not a measure of what others think of you but what you think of yourself. Codependents suffer from lower levels of self-esteem, and thus they seek validation from others. They feel bad or good, depending on other things and even other people.

Whenever you become a winner in a competition or complete all your deadlines, you feel that immense joy and satisfaction. You know that feeling, right? Well, that is the same exact feeling that people with high self-esteem have at all times of the day. But in the case of most people, whenever they face some setback, be it financial or emotional, they feel at a loss, but all these feelings are short-lived, and they will not last forever. You also have to keep in mind that they do not reflect your self-esteem. External events don't have the power to affect good self-esteem. When people have high self-esteem, they realize that external events are merely transient, and they can in no way reflect them as a person. So, they do not get affected by these events.

But, in the case of people with low self-esteem, they feel disappointment and immense loss. They feel as if they have lost everything they had. This is mostly the case with codependent people because of their low self-esteem. They rely on external factors like prestige, beauty, money, or maybe appreciation from others for their self-worth. But, in reality, none of this can actually affect your self-esteem if you do not let them. If what you are doing is solely based on the fact that you want the approval of others, then it is not self-esteem even if you think highly of yourself. This is because every feeling that you have is heavily dependent on what others think of you.

The inherent nature of codependent people is to depend on others, and because of this, they are not connected to their own selves. They fail to follow their inner guidance, and self-trust is something they find difficult to achieve. They are always at a loss when it comes to making up their mind regarding something, and they always rely on others to make their decisions for them. They are unsure of what they really want in a particular situation, and this promotes them to defer to others to seek love and appreciation. Codependent people can also be super-critical, and thus they end up finding some kind of flaw with everything related to them. It can be the way they think or look or basically everything in day to day life. They do not realize how widespread their self-judgment has become.

Codependent people are super-sensitive to criticism, and when they do receive some compliments, they try to run away from the situation because they think that they do not deserve all that love. And this same feeling of being self-critical makes them criticize others heavily. But you must not worry as all of this is learned, and anything that is learned can also be unlearned with consistent practice.

Being a People Pleaser

One of the biggest signs that you are a people pleaser is if you try to change yourself completely in order to accommodate another person. This type of behavior arises from the fact that these people want others to validate their presence. Codependents are never able to center their world around themselves. They always want someone else to appreciate them, need them, or love them. If you are trying your best to accommodate others by becoming a people pleaser yourself, then you are in a codependent relationship.

People pleasers always seek acceptance from others, and if by any chance, someone becomes unhappy with them, they start feeling anxious. They start giving others precedence over their own needs, and the thoughts and feelings of others gain more importance in their life. They start molding themselves in every way possible so that they become someone they think is acceptable to the people around them. This is even more commonly seen in romantic relationships. They try to be perfect all the time and fit in, do well, be the responsible one, or look good. This leads to further shame, and they start hiding every wound.

You will become more and more estranged from your true self, the more you rely on external factors to measure your feelings. All of this enhances the addition to others or the need to cling to someone else and seek validation. This is something very similar to how an addict reacts to a drug and takes it despite knowing the fact that the drug is going to do nothing but harm. The drug then starts feeling every kind of void they feel in life.

You need to remember that pleasing others does not have any long-term benefits. It might bring you some temporary relief, but that is it. The more you rely on others, the more your addiction will grow up to a point when you become completely dependent on the other person. The problem of people-pleasing usually starts in childhood. Children often fall prey to the thought that accommodating every wish and need of their parents is what will make them the perfect child or help them navigate through this world. They also think that accommodating is the only way in which they can win their parents' love.

They start correlating being 'good' to something that their parents want. Now, parents, on the other hand, usually have high expectations or rigid rules or might even punish the child if he/she is not able to keep up with what they want. This lowers the self-esteem of the child and forces them to become a people pleaser for their entire life.

People pleasers develop a mentality in which they think that they are not lovable the way they are. Codependents display this same behavior. They start becoming compliant because they think that will bring them, love, from others. They start rejecting all those character traits that they think will disappoint others. They can even start eliminating character traits just because they want to fit in.

Guilt

You must be thinking that guilt and shame are the same two things, but they are not. Shame is a feeling that a person has about oneself, and this feeling is not good, whereas guilt is something related to what you have done or said that is below your standards and maybe violating your ethical principle. In the case of codependents, this feeling of guilt gets tapped deep into shame, and together it becomes a magnified feeling that is hard to get rid of. If you are guilty, then you might have thoughts that begin something like, 'I should not have said that.' But soon enough, you might even feel shame as in 'I am rude and selfish.'

Sometimes, guilt can get accumulated and become compounded to an amount that it is too much to handle. It can rob you of your peace of mind. You have to know that you are human and by that, I mean to say that you too have feelings. But in the case of codependents, feelings are something they are ashamed of and feel guilty about. They judge their own feelings and keep wondering what is normal. They feel guilt boiling inside them when they are angry, and they keep telling themselves that they shouldn't be feeling the way they do. When they are depressed, they feel that something is wrong with them, whereas it's not. They have some perceived mistakes in their minds, and

22

from time to time, they keep reviewing past conversations and actions to feel guilt from these so-called mistakes.

The several negative emotions and thoughts of codependency can cloud your actual self. A very common sign seen in those who have just suffered a breakup is that they will continually think about where they had gone wrong. They will try in every way possible to adapt themselves to their partner because they think accommodating others will win them over. They feel guilty about what they need and thus do not assert them as well. They always judge themselves to be indulgent, weak, and selfish. Codependents have this tendency to think that their needs are burdensome, and thus, they cannot ask others for their help.

Another thing that is noticed in codependents is that they also feel guilty about what others are feeling. For example, they might go to a movie together with their spouse but end up blaming themselves in case their spouse doesn't like the movie. They do not know how to disagree about keeping their guilt at bay.

They cow away from facing their partner regarding that person's behaviors, and they always keep thinking that it is they who need to be guilty of what the other person has done. They blamed themselves even when the fault wasn't theirs in the first place. They feel so undeserving and unworthy that they literally attract punishment. They even end up accepting the unjust way others treat them just because they think that they deserve all that harsh treatment.

Pursuing Perfectionism

There is nothing called perfection in this world, and yet people crave it madly. It is nothing but an illusion that is present in other people's minds. It is also something that is out of reach. But those who tend to be the perfectionists are never sure of what things are good for them. They always think that they are failures because they couldn't keep up with their own expectations. They indulge in a constant battle with their own selves, and they have unrealistic self-comparison. This, in turn, leads to a continual phase of self-shaming and self-judgment. And all of this is not only applicable to any particular incident in their life but their entire self.

The combination of guilt, shame, and perfectionism can be quite self-defeating. This becomes even more challenging in situations when you are seeking love from someone who is not willing to give it or has the ability to impart love only in bits and pieces. This makes you try harder every time, and you want to do your best so that you can prove that you are lovable.   This not only quells your inner feelings of shame but only assists in self-validation.

On the other hand, there are certain types of codependents whose only task is to prove that they are worthy, and they do this through their accomplishments. They always think that they are flawed in some way or the other, and this leads to internalized shame. There are some perfectionists who become the way they are because of shame. The most common example of this is someone who always aims to get an A in a test. This kind of perfectionism is usual because that person will feel ashamed if they get anything less than an A, but there are other students as well who don't aim anything at all because they think that they are hopeless failures anyway.

Another common example is when a woman thinks that everything related to her has to be spotless. She has taken the idea up to such a point that she even wants her home to be spotless. Her environment is also affected by her shame. She sees everything in her life as a reflection of herself, which she considers to be flawed. Whenever something is out of place or dusty in her surroundings, she instantly correlates it to anxiety. And most of the time, these kinds of people can fix their feelings only when they fix their surroundings and not in any way else.

The biggest myth about perfectionism is that some people think it helps build self-esteem, whereas it's just quite the opposite. Perfectionists are neither hard-working nor goal-driven. They are simply fed up with the fact that they have to keep trying in order to become perfect constantly. Their feelings of isolation or shame intensify too. There should be a proper balance between self-acceptance and self-improvement, and only then can you realize that self-worth is not something that you can earn overtime.

Dysfunctional Boundaries

Your self-esteem is reflected in your boundaries. Your boundaries are what demarcates your feelings from that of others. And this is also how you embody your individual self. When you are aware of your boundaries, you will know that when you should not be violating others' boundaries and how you can protect yourself from others. But the importance of boundaries is inculcated in the childhood years. If someone is not taught, then he/she ends up disrespecting others and is not aware when they are being inappropriate. Violating someone's boundary will feel casual to them if their parents used to violate their boundaries as a child.

Boundaries are of four different types—material, physical, emotional, and mental. Material boundaries are those which involve the distribution and sharing of your money and possessions. People who fail to put up the essential boundaries will not practice any amount of discretion when they give a loan. If someone borrows money from a person without taking permission from him/her or fails to return it on time, then that person has zero respect for the boundaries of others.

Physical boundaries are the ones that are more intimately associated with your body. These boundaries are the ones that decide when or whom you allow to touch you or invade your personal space. While growing up, if proper privacy is not given to a child or if they are not given the necessary control over their own bodies, then it is a violation of their physical boundary. A very common way of understanding the physical boundaries of a person is by monitoring how close they are standing to you or even by a kiss or hug. In case someone tries to persist in doing something physical even after you have shown signs of denial, then that person is violating your physical boundary.

When someone has suffered from incidences of sexual or physical abuse in their childhood years, then they either develop a very weak boundary in their later life or have a non-existent physical boundary. Provocative language, flirtation, or inappropriate nudity can also be acts of violation of someone's boundary. Spouses often face conflicts on various matters because their boundaries are not the same. This is the result of a different upbringing on each of their parts. Some of the common examples of such conflicts are related to sharing money, locking doors, or sharing personal belongings.

Then we move on to the topic of emotional boundaries. These are more difficult to understand as they are not prominent. Your emotional boundaries define your emotional responsibilities and rights. When you are in an intimate relationship with someone else, you must have a healthy emotional boundary because only then will you be able to preserve yourself. When your boundaries are healthy, the sense of self and emotional identity of every person remains clear.

Then there are mental boundaries, which are those that are related to your beliefs and opinions. These boundaries prevent you from becoming dogmatic and stick to your opinions even in the face of a challenge. But those who were not allowed to make their own decisions in their childhood years do not have proper mental boundaries. They tend to become angry in every argument that they are a part of. These reactions arise from those times in their life when parents or elders had silenced or criticized their views.

When someone is codependent, they lack these boundaries. They are unable to name their feelings or separate theirs from others'. With poor emotional boundaries, codependents tend to make the problem of others their own, and they start taking responsibility for it. In some cases, for example, if the partner has sexual dysfunction, the codependent person might even blame himself/herself for that.

Too Much Dependence

Codependents have this tendency to invest their own self in others way too much. In this process, they lose their own selves. They do not care about their hobbies, feelings, goals, or needs. Their entire life starts revolving around the needs and wishes of someone else. By definition of the term, you will notice that codependents are 'dependents.' They have this nagging habit of valuing someone else's wishes or opinions more than their own. They even fail to make their own decisions. They even have a constant fear that people will leave them or reject them, and due to this, they not only feel sad or depressed, but they also feel inadequate.

Codependents also face difficulty in starting any new projects on their own. In case they are in a relationship, they feel they have been trapped in that bond and that they cannot escape it even if they want to. They start focusing all their time and energy on others and then gradually give up on their own well-being. They do not keep any separate time for their personal growth. Even if someone is hurting them, they stay loyal to that person instead of breaking free from such a toxic relationship. If the codependents are single, then they are usually always in search of someone so that the other person can make them happy. And if they are in a relationship, they spend all their time trying to make that person happy.

They become so overly invested in others that they are hardly content with their own selves. They start depending on that other person so much that they start using them to fill the gaps in their own life. And in doing this, they reach a certain point in their life where they start getting controlled by the other person, and their feelings and thoughts get

28

influenced by that other person as well. They sometimes even try to get control over the other person so that their feelings and needs are honored. In some ways, they can even become manipulative or get manipulated.

Fear of Rejection

When one partner in a relationship is codependent, then he/she always bear the fear of being left alone or being rejected. There are some who fear to sleep alone. You will never feel whole if you are not connected to your soul. So, when the codependent person fails to cater to their own needs, they always feel that someone else will swoop in and satisfy them. They might share a good bond with a lot of people, but no relationship in their life could fill the gaps. Even when they are in love with someone and in a relationship with that person, they feel alone. And when they start being attached to that person, that same relationship becomes an addiction to them.

When a person has faced abandonment in their childhood years, they suffer from problems of insecurity and low self-esteem. They worry about whether or not they can count on others and whether they are loved. Sometimes all of this results in shame anxiety. This feeling leads to apprehension about being rejected. In some cases, the person may even imagine rejection, whereas, in reality, there is nothing like that. Abandonment doesn't always have to be complete isolation due to divorce or death. Sometimes, the parents are not emotionally available for their child, and this is also a case of abandonment.

Sustained abandonment creates an unworthy feeling in the child, and he/she starts to think that they are not enough the way they are and that they always have to give their full energy in order to accommodate others. They always indulge in people-pleasing out of fear of rejection. They try to hide their flaws, and in worst scenarios, they even end up tolerating abuse. They do all of this just because they do not want others to leave them.

Chapter 3:

How People Become Codependent?

As you must have already gathered until now, codependency is all about sacrificing the needs of your own and giving someone else more important than yourself. Codependent people focus entirely on people around them and not on their own needs. Their life is unhealthy and unbalanced. But how does someone become codependent in the first place? According to research, nature develops mostly due to the pattern of childhood upbringing, and it is explained in detail in this chapter. If you have already diagnosed your traits of codependency, it is very common for you to wonder where they came from. You might also be wondering why it is so difficult to come out of such a codependent relationship. Well, the answers to these questions usually vary from person to person. But, as already mentioned above, most of the reasons will point to the childhood of the person. This is because, in childhood years, humans are more impressionable. Life experiences or cognitive abilities are not present at that age, and so kids fail to realize which emotional attachments are healthy and which are not. They do not understand that what their parents are saying is not always right. Parents, thus, manipulate and lie to their child and fail to provide a healthy and secure attachment.

Link Between Codependency and Childhood Emotional Neglect

Do you feel disconnected and empty from within but yet cannot specify what exactly is wrong with you? Well, you should know that Childhood Emotional Neglect or CEN is something that should not be taken lightly. It is very powerful but often remains untreated. It is often found that even those who have been the victims of CEN labeled their childhood to be good because they failed to realize that something was wrong in it. The person you are today has a lot to do with your upbringing. Your childhood is what shapes you. All the emotional and physical needs of a child are fulfilled by his/her parents. But when parents are not able to fulfill this task, a significant amount of damage is done, and this is often invisible. When a parent fails to respond or adequately validate the emotional needs of a child, that is when CEN happens. Now, this is something a person fails to notice even when they are adults because CEN is not about what happened. It is more about what did not happen. There are no scars or bruises but only void and confusion. Here is an example of how an emotionally neglectful family looks like. If the child came back from school sad because he wasn't selected for the school football team and then wanted to speak to his mother, who then shooed him away, then the child has no one to talk to. And then to increase the grief, the grandpa might tell him not to cry because it is not expected from a boy. No one from the family helped the kid process his feelings, and thus he was not physically neglected but emotionally. In some cases, CEN occurs in addition to physical abuse, and these situations are common in those households where the parent is an addict or is mentally ill.

33

But you will find several children who are victims of CEN but didn't face any obvious dysfunction in their family. They were not belittled or abused. They had parents who wanted them to do well but lacked the skills necessary to build emotional contact. Such parents are unaware of the ways in which they can attend to their child's feelings. These children grow up and become adults, and they might show that they have gotten it all together, but in reality, they are alone, and they have a void. They cannot fit in, but at the same time, there is nothing visibly wrong on the outside.

The person that you are today is hugely formed by your feelings. So, when your feelings are not validated or noticed, you start feeling that you are no longer important to others. Growing up in an emotionally neglectful family makes the child think that feelings are an inconvenience and so they should not be entertained. So, they start developing this tendency of pushing their feelings away from a young age or shoving them to a corner by taking the help of drugs, alcohol, food, or sex. Your internal state of self will remain unacknowledged until and unless you take care of your emotional needs. You will start displaying needy or clingy behaviors and always seek others' attention because you will want to prove your worth. You will be overworked in an attempt to find perfectionism. But the solution to your problem does not lie with external validation because they can never fill the void within.

When you do not have enough emotional attachment, you will find it difficult in your life to understand others, for example, your own children or spouse. When children face CEN, they are constantly told that it is they who are to blame for the problem, or sometimes they are told that there is no problem at all. But all of this makes life confusing for the

34

child because he/she can feel that something is wrong in their life. As a result of this, they gradually start making peace with the fact that they are the problem and thus start thinking of themselves as inadequate, incapable, and stupid. This belief, in turn, leads to codependent relationships in adults.

What is the Effect of CEN or Childhood Emotional Neglect?

When children are subjected to CEN, they develop certain habits, or several things can happen, which are listed below:

You Develop Caretaking Habits

In the childhood years, when parents were neglecting and didn't cater to the needs of the child, it promotes the child to become the parent to their own selves. Thus, they start developing caretaking habits. This helps them to fill the gaps that no one helped them fill. But what helped then in their childhood years didn't prove to be of much help when they grew up and instead acted in the opposite manner. When a person grows up in a troubled environment, they get confused between love and pain. Love isn't supposed to be hurtful, even if relationships meant conflicts and disappointment. But a codependent person has the inherent habit of neglecting their own needs and putting others in the first place. That is how they end up self-sacrificing. They think that love means they have to be the caretaker to the other person.

The relationship gets negatively influenced by caretaking as the codependent person treats the other person like a child who doesn't have to grow up ever.

You Come to Realize That People Who Claim to Love You Can Also Hurt Your Feelings

Children who face CEN are used to an upbringing where their parents had abandoned them, lied to them, never cared for their feelings, and in some cases, might have even threatened them. Such emotionally neglectful parents don't think twice before taking advantage of your kindness. You become so used to these things that this is what the idea of a family becomes to you. Gradually when you grow up, you let everyone come into your life and hurt you. You let your friends and lover take advantage of your nature while you give them more priority over yourself.

You Become a People Pleaser

CEN promotes the person to always try and be in control, and they do this by keeping others happy and becoming a people pleaser. They do not disagree or speak up because of fear that the other person might leave them. They keep giving so much that there is nothing left for themselves. They spend all their energy and love on others, and thus, at the end of the day, they are so exhausted that they do not have anything left for themselves. They derive a strange emotional fulfillment by helping others, even if it means putting their own interests in danger. This also subsequently feeds their self-worth.

They are so much preoccupied with what others are feeling and thinking about then. They have this overdeveloped sense of responsibility that they think the mistakes of others are also a mess that they have to clean. Thus, when people who have faced CEN grow up to become codependents, they get stuck in relationships where they mostly exhaust themselves by giving away too much and do not get anything

36

in return. But the beginning of people-pleasing is usually with parent-pleasing. In childhood, they develop this behavior in order to keep their parents happy or maintain closeness with them so that the parents give them some amount of attention.

You Cannot Form Healthy Boundaries

When children are brought up in a household where no one pays much attention to them, they are unable to learn how to set up healthy boundaries. So, they either set up boundaries that are fragile and all wrong, or they have too rigid boundaries. When people have weak boundaries, they feel alone and vulnerable.

When they are in a close relationship with someone, they tend to lose themselves. They start indulging in sexual relationships with strangers, get into physical relationships very easily, and do not know how to say 'no' and so end up saying 'yes' to practically everything in life. They reveal their inner self and privacies to people who they have met for literally a few minutes, and thus, they start trusting people all too easily. When boundaries are nonexistent or blurry, relationships can become messy and scary.

On the contrary, some people tend to have too rigid boundaries, and they consider it their arsenal for self-protection. They get into relationships with inflexible rules, and they have this tendency to get isolated in every place.

They avoid intimacy at all costs because that makes them vulnerable. Sometimes trauma is also the reason behind rigid boundaries that are being carried on from childhood.

37

You Always Feel Guilty

As codependents who have faced CEN, guilt is a constant companion. Such people set unrealistic expectations that are hard to fulfill, and thus, they are tormented when the expectations are not met. They are sensitive to all types of criticism that they turn to people-pleasing as a saving mechanism. Due to this guilt, people are unable to detach themselves from negative people, and this, in turn, adds to the problem of codependents. They have some set roles in life that they have accepted since their childhood years, and they think that it is impossible to break out of these roles. Practicing self-care also makes them guilty because they think that they are being selfish.

The very basis of guilt is based on the fact that you think you are doing something wrong, even when you are doing it right. This is a tormenting situation. Codependents result from CEN when they constantly keep beating themselves up for mistakes they didn't make. The habit of feeling responsible for others' actions is also one of the reasons why codependents face so much guilt.

You Have Fear Tormenting You

Being constantly neglected since childhood instills a fear that carries on with you to your adulthood. Since CEN lowers your self-esteem, several types of fears become deeply rooted in your mind, and some of them are that of abandonment, intimacy, rejection, power, criticism, and even failure. The number of fears in a person who is a victim of CEN is way more than any normal person, and these fears are also one of the reasons why they become codependent later on. The fear also leads to anxiety, which means they start apprehending threats that might crop up in the future.

38

With anxiety comes powerlessness and unpredictability. Humans have been made to respond to every crisis situation with a fight or flee attitude. But you cannot do anything about some situations, and that is what leads to anxiety. That is also when people start projecting their fears and thoughts on others and end up sabotaging their own relationships.

When a kid is brought up in a family that keeps on quarreling or bad-mouthing one another, the kid grows up to dread every family occasion because he/she fears that it will become a complete disappointment by turning into a battleground. So, they grow up to try and control everything so that they can prevent such situations from happing. That is how a codependent is born.

You Cannot Trust Anyone

People who have faced CEN have been treated badly and have been betrayed over and over again by their own loved ones. That is why they cannot trust anyone ever again when they become adults. On the other hand, trust is the cornerstone of any healthy relationship, but when that trust cannot be conveyed by one partner, the relationship is no longer healthy, and the partner becomes codependent. The partners are not able to discuss every aspect openly or be true about their feelings. Communication is often defensive, indirect, and reactive. There are so many misunderstandings and doubts that crop up just because you do not have enough trust among yourselves.

Keeping secrets, lying, and breaking promises worsens the situation even more. With CEN, people often try to predict the behaviors of people, and when something goes out of line, it raises doubt and mistrust. The lack of trust in

39

relationships leads you to take matters into your own hands and babysit your partner, which is one of the core reasons for codependency.

You Are Depressed and in Despair

Depression and long-term exposure to despair are two of the very common reasons behind a person becoming codependent. These feelings result in hopelessness, and the person struggles with recovery too. There is always an unending feeling of crises in their life that they can't figure out. They feel lonely and abandoned by everyone in their life. Their needs are never met because they were neglected in their childhood and became a codependent individual, so now they give more priority to others.

They are in a situation where they feel as if every feeling has been taken away from them. When depression leads to codependency, the person enters into a cycle where they try to hide the depression with a busy schedule, dramatic relationships, or anything that involves an adrenalin rush. But when it all calms down, the depression starts to resurface, and the person again tries to bring some sort of drama into his/her life.

You Feel Resentment and Anger

With people breaking promises constantly and hurting your feelings since childhood, it is very natural to develop anger and resentment. Due to these feelings, people often become codependent and take control over every relationship in their lives. Codependents who have also faced CEN often feel trapped and relationships start seeming burdensome. They keep loving the people in their lives who cause all the sadness. They feel guilty to simply leave their loved ones.

40

When people don't acknowledge their anger, it often starts bottling up and ultimately bursts leading to expression in the wrong manners. When anger remains unexpressed for a long time, it turns into resentment. When people have unhealthy role models in their childhood years with both or either of the parents being aggressive, the child grows up to have serious anger issues. You need to channel your rage into something good in order to get out of the cycle.

All these unresolved issues that are mentioned above gets carried on to your adulthood and changes your relationship dynamics. You do not understand the distinction between healthy and unhealthy relationships and end up giving up on codependency. As a child, you had to undergo such neglectful behavior; you come up with ways of your own that help you to cope with your day to day life. Then you start thinking that your codependent traits are what helps you adapt to your current state in life. You start looking at your codependent traits in a compassionate light. If your parents were not able to cater to your needs, it does not mean that you are imperfect or flawed. You do not need to spend your entire life thinking that if you do not try your best to please others, they will not stay. You don't have to stay that scared little child forever. You need to break free from your cocoon and see the world around you.

You must have noticed by now that codependency does not happen in one day and that it is mostly a learned behavior. Children have the habit of depending on their parents, but parents are not always dependable, and that is what hurts the kid and makes him/her emotionally wounded. This hurt has to be healed and confronted; otherwise, the child will grow up to be in the same situation as his/her parents. Codependency is stemmed from love, and there are healthy ways in which you can overcome it. But if you cannot detach yourself at the right time, then you will have to endure a rollercoaster ride with your partner.

When children do not receive the attention they deserve, they often grow up to ignore their own feelings. They start suppressing all their thoughts and needs. When no one pays attention to them, they start thinking about what use would it be to bother about expressing their needs and feelings. In extreme cases, it also happens that the child shuts himself/herself off because they fear they will be punished for speaking up. Since parents fail to take up any kind of responsibility whatsoever, the children start blaming themselves for everything wrong and take responsibility for their parents' mistakes. This behavior torments them for their entire life, and all their future relationships are plagued by this. They ignore their own feelings and start feeling responsible for the action of others.

Traumatic childhood experiences, thus, definitely play a big role in turning a person towards codependency as a coping mechanism. But recovery is possible, as is discussed in the latter part of this book.

Chapter 4:

How to Overcome Denial in Codependency?

Denial is a very important aspect of codependency, and you have to learn how to overcome it. This chapter is all about it, and it is impossible to overcome codependency if you do not face your problems and go past the phase of denial. Here you will first learn the types of denial and then some tips to deal with it.

Why Do People Go into Denial?

The reason why people go into denial is pretty simple. People set it up as a defense mechanism. The first line of defense that your brain sets up for any crises that come your way is denial. No one does it on purpose. It happens unconsciously. The brain will actually put it in front of you in such a manner that it will seem non-threatening to you at the time. Subsequently, you alter the way you see things so that you are protected against getting hurt or overwhelmed. Here are some of the common reasons why people prefer to be in denial—

To Avoid Difficult Emotions

Codependents go into denial to avoid any feelings or thoughts that might lead to pain if they were asked to come face to face with the facts of your life. Everyone is wired to

44

sort to denial in order to survive. You will often find children denying their actions because they fear punishment, and thus, they deny out of self-preservation.

An example of where denial is used to mask difficult emotions is when someone close to you meets death. Those few days after the incident, you will be in immense grief, and you will move into denial, especially if the separation was sudden and out of the blue. When people move into denial, they find it easier to cope with the shock. But denial is not healthy, especially if you are delaying something important. For example, some women may not go for mammograms at the right time just because they fear the outcome. But delaying the process might worsen the situation altogether.

To Avoid Inner Conflict

The second reason is to avoid any sort of conflict either with yourself or with someone you love that involves making some difficult choices and hurting someone in the process. This type of conflict is very common in children who are powerless to leave their homes and thus go into denial about their emotions.

Children have the habit of idealizing their parents, but sometimes, it can turn out to be unhealthy. They cannot think of the unthinkable that it is their parents who are at fault. So, they do the alternative. They start blaming themselves for everything that is happening.

In the case of adults, they go into denial because they don't want to make the decisions that would lead to some sort of conflict. For example, if a person has a huge debt to pay, then he/she might completely shove the thought out of their mind because they do not want the debt to affect their standard of living. They go into denial to avoid the chance of abandonment, loss, emotional or physical harm, death, or serious illness

Due to Familiarity

Another common reason that people, especially codependents, go into denial is that they are familiar with the situation. They have grown up facing the same things, and they have endured those conditions. So, they do not think anything is wrong with it. For example, if a person were abused emotionally as a child, then he/she would not consider mistreatment by the spouse as an act of abuse. Also, if someone was molested in their childhood, then it is likely that they would go into denial about their child getting incested.

At most, they might end up acknowledging the fact that the spouse is being verbally abusive. But somehow or the other, they would try to rationalize the situation. When victims move on to third-degree denial, they completely shut their eyes to the detrimental effect the abuse is having on them. So, eventually, the victim suffers from PTSD.

As a Coping Mechanism After Trauma

Some codependents also resort to denial because it helps them deal with some trauma that resulted due to abuse, which might have happened recently or a long time ago. People don't realize how big a role shame plays in the lives of everyone. Feelings and needs are often shame-bonded right from the childhood years. So, codependents take up denial towards their own feelings, and thus, their needs are not met.

46

What Are the Types of Denial?

Denial is not at all healthy when it comes to codependency. When you run away from your problems or hide, you are not able to learn the several constructive mechanisms that you can put to use to come out of the codependent way of life. The different types of denial faced by codependents are explained below—

Denial of Behavior

The first one is where you are denying the fact that the behavior shown by someone or that person's actions is affecting you negatively. This happens in codependents because they might have grown up in a family where such behavior was normalized. Sometimes, acknowledging the fact that is right in front of you can cause conflicts with your inner self and lead to shame. That is why people stay in denial. For example, if you are in love with someone who shows addictive behavior, then you can either address those issues or choose to be in denial of the repercussions of their behavior. You don't have to think about the negative effects of that person's behavior in your life. If your lover is into gambling and you are in denial about it, then you don't have to worry about going bankrupt because you are not addressing the fact to be of serious concern. But you need to understand something. Denial is not about staying unaffected by someone's behavior. Rather, it is about not labeling the actions for what they are and masking them under false pretenses, and creating fantasies.

This kind of behavior is very common when a person doesn't want to accept the fact that their partner has some serious addictive behavior or mental problem that needs to be addressed. But with denial, things don't become better. Instead, they get worse.

Denial of Codependency

When confronted about their habits, codependents have the habit of completely denying their codependent attitude. They think that whatever they are doing is the only way out of the situation and that there is no other way to do it. They portray the situation in a way as if they have no other choice. But it is not that. They do have a choice, and they chose to help the other person over themselves. They do this to avoid any deeper pain. If you are still confused about whether you are a codependent person or not, then you should check out Chapter 2, where I have outlined all the signs of a codependent personality.

Another reason that plays a role in the denial of codependency is the fact that codependents are not used to looking at themselves. They have always been focused on others their entire life. They do not know how they can take responsibility for their own marriage. They are always running towards a fruitless goal where they want to change others or make them happy. They do this because they are under the false illusion that their happiness is derived from these external sources or by making others happy. They avoid self-examination by feeling superior or blaming others. For example, Sara has been looking for the perfect man for a long time but not getting one. She thinks that the perfect man is going to suddenly come into her life and make everything all bright and sunny. But she blames that the lack of good men is what has promoted her unsuccessful relationships, thereby denying her codependent behavior altogether.

Denial of How They Feel

Codependents are aware of what people around them are feeling, and they also start worrying about those people. When they are obsessed with someone else's feelings or even with some material things like drugs or food or alcohol, they use that to mask their own feelings and steer clear of confronting them. If you ask a codependent how he or she is feeling, the answer that you are going to get most likely would be 'I'm fine.' That's all they have to say, even when everything is not fine.

They are in an endless loop of denial about their feelings. They can only understand physical pain but not the pain that results from emotions. This is because while growing up, they weren't taught to acknowledge their true feelings, or when they tried expressing them, they didn't feel safe. So, eventually, they shut themselves off and went into denial about what they are truly feeling. When they are in denial, their pain from repressed feelings keeps accumulating over the years. Denial of feelings also brings about inappropriate reactions to situations and, in turn, creates more problems.

Denial of Their Own Needs

Codependents have the habit of always trying to fulfill the needs of others and forgetting their own needs in the process. While growing up, if the codependent person was neglected, then the physical needs of that person were never taken care of. Alternatively, if he/she was raised in an abusive household, they never felt safe, and now, they don't realize that it is a prerequisite of all relationships. So, if you ask a codependent about his/her needs, whereas all their life, they were shamed or abused for it, then it will be similar to ask a blind person what is present in front of them.

49

Codependents usually learn how to be self-sufficient in life, and this is because no one ever took care of them as a child. Their emotional needs were denied right at their faces. Even if some of them are aware of their needs, they feel humiliated to ask for help from someone else.

How to Get Started With the Process of Overcoming Denial?

If you want to get rid of codependency, then the first step is to break free of denial. This is the first step to recovery. But you should not underestimate the patience, time, and attention that is required in the process. All of these qualities can back you up even when the times are hard. But reading and thinking about the steps to recovery in your mind will never be enough. You have to place your commitment that you will recover and break free from this phase of denial. If you want to change, you really have to want to do so. Yes, there will be moments when you will be asking yourself whether all this effort is worth, but trust me, it is.

But, first, you need to understand that overcoming denial involves change. Any kind of recovery starts with change and so you need to embrace it. Change brings new possibilities and paves the path for personal growth. It is way more than simply changing your habitual routine. It also means trying your hand at new endeavors, including behaviors, attitudes, beliefs, and perceptions.

Some of the common barriers that will come your way are mentioned below so that you can be aware of them and not let them stop you from recovering.

- In order to survive, you might have already taken some of your own measures to get used to the difficult circumstances. That entire process of adapting could have been painful, and so you might not want to change again out of fear that it will bring you more pain than you could not possibly bear.

- Sometimes, codependents make repeated attempts at breaking free from the phase of denial but are not quite successful at it. So, after a certain point in time, they become overwhelmed and give up. But you need to keep at it constantly if you want to succeed. The constant attempt to control the uncontrollable things or the gravity of your current situation in life might act as a barrier to change.

- It is a typical habit of codependents to want others to make them happy. They do not want to take the responsibility themselves and always want someone else to do it for them. So, they will definitely want things to change and complain about the situation too, but they won't do anything about it because they want to depend on someone else to do it for them.

- Sometimes, they see change as a form of threat. Greater fear accompanies with bigger and graver decisions. They fear standing up to intimidation; they fear abandonment, and they also fear the unknown.

- Along with the bad days, you will also have good days, and in those good days, you might simply want to set aside the necessity to change.

If you want to change, it also means that you have to start becoming responsible for your contributions. Whatever happens tomorrow, be it good or bad, you have to hold yourself responsible for it. You also need to understand who the change is for. It is for yourself and not for someone else. Codependents are so used to doing things for others that they think the process of recovery is also an action they are taking for someone else's benefit. But it is not. It is for your sole benefit. If you cannot understand the fact that at the end of the day, it is only you, then you will not be able to start walking on the path of change.

Codependency has this toxic quality of robbing its victims of their contentment, vibrancy, and health. Don't let it happen to you. Yes, it will be difficult to put yourself first because all your life, you are used to catering to the needs of others. You are habituated to making other the priority in your life and not yourself. But you will get through it. When someone learns a new skill, do they learn it in one single day? No, right? It is the same with you. If you want to bring about a change, you have to practice daily without losing hope, and you will definitely get around it.

Also, if you want to break free from your denial, there is no shame in seeking some help and support. It will help you stay true to your path even when you are distracted or dissuaded. You will get encouragement, information, and validation that you so badly need. Your support will keep reminding you of your ultimate goal, and this will help you stay focused on your path.

You have to challenge all your underlying assumptions about life. You need to stop burying your feelings and your problems. There will be discomfort because you are handling something new for the first time, but it is all normal, and if you have support by your side, he/she will keep you motivated so that your codependent self cannot sabotage your recovery.

Chapter 5:

How to Build Self-Esteem and Indulge in Self-Love to Overcome Codependency?

Have you ever seen a garden that is left neglected? There will be weeds and growing here and there. It is the same with your self-esteem. It has to be nurtured from your childhood years if you want it to prosper. Figure out all those thoughts and feelings which are playing a role in undermining your self-esteem. That is the first step towards realizing your self-worth and indulging in self-love.

This chapter deals with how you can build your self-esteem and also practice self-love because both of these actions will help you overcome codependency.

Re-Educate Your Inner Critic

Everyone has an inner critic, and codependents have a very strong one. This inner voice constantly points out all your shortcomings and mistakes. This voice can act as a healthy conscience if you want it to. But, in most cases, your inner critic can lower your levels of self-esteem by giving you an overdose of self-criticism. You might feel insecure because your self-critic will constantly undermine your ambition and confidence in life. You will also feel vagueness, not enough, or inadequate. So, if you, as a codependent, are finding it difficult to pursue your goals, it is probably because your inner critic is always pulling strings.

Your inner critic's intentions are never bad. It always tries to protect you from anything bad. But sometimes this protection is exactly what you don't need as you need to go out and see the world for yourself. If left uncontrolled, your inner critic will soon become the relentless fault-finder. So, you need to re-educate it. The first step is to recognize your inner voice. For that, you need to sit quietly without being disturbed and focus on the thoughts that you are having. Start making a list of all the negative thoughts you are having or all those things you hate about yourself. You will find your inner critic stating some criticisms throughout the day, and you need to be on the lookout for those and jot them down the moment they crop up in your mind.

If there are any signs of negative thinking, try thinking backward and trace those thoughts to their origin, that is, the incident that triggered those thoughts in the first place. You also need to examine the tone and voice of your inner critic. Does it have a close resemblance to someone in your life or in your past? If yes, then it is probably the words of someone in your childhood, most likely your parents, who left such a huge impact that you have grown to internalize all that shame and anger.

Now that you have identified your inner critic, it is time to reframe your thinking process. For every negative thought, come up with a positive alternative and be your own supportive coach.

Don't Be a Slave to the 'Pusher' in Your Mind

Just like the inner critic, everyone has a 'Pusher' inside their minds, which pushes them to take up more than they can handle. So, if that 'Pusher' voice in your head urges you to get more things done, you don't necessarily have to listen to it. You don't have to become a slave to complete your to-do lists. Do your work at your own pace. It is also true that the 'Pusher' is only looking forward to making you better at what you do, but sometimes there is too much to do, and the time is less. So, taking up too much work only makes you stressed.

The 'Pusher' never lets you stay at peace with yourself. Even if you are relaxing, this same 'Pusher' will urge you to take action on a dozen things in your life that are still unfinished. The 'Pusher,' along with your inner critic, joins hands to make your life miserable. The only way to break free from this mentality is to take a short vacation from time to time. Keep track of when you are becoming anxious and take small breaks to release the pent-up stress.

Accept Imperfection

As a codependent, you have to understand that there is nothing called perfectionism, and everyone is imperfect. Once you have understood this fact, the next step is to accept your imperfections and love them. When a codependent thinks that he/she is not perfect, it results in shame, which starts accumulating in their minds. Gradually, they start fearing rejection by others in their life. If you think about it carefully, then you will understand that perfectionism is driven by nothing other than shame. When you are a

56

perfectionist, you tend to focus all your energy on your inabilities and mistakes. At the core of your heart, you think that you are not adequate for everything in your life.

Some people resort to perfectionism because they want to escape all the pain in their life. Ultimately, this leads to a condition where you are not able to finish any of your tasks at hand out of fear of being imperfect. The inner critic does the constant judgment of your actions and urges you to meet the unrealistic expectations and standards that you have constructed in your mind. So, do you know what the antidote to this kind of behavior is? Well, it is self-acceptance. The moment you start accepting yourself for the person you are, half of your problems will be solved. If you do not accept yourself, you cannot really change because then you will be in constant conflict with your reality.

A practice that you can inculcate is that you can make a list of all the thoughts and beliefs you have about yourself and your life. Then you need to ask yourself, why do you think you are not enough? There will definitely be some things that you don't love. It might be something to do with your appearance or with your actions. Then, you need to tell yourself, 'I accept myself because…' and in this way, you will be reframing your negative beliefs with positive ones. The moment you let go of your mistaken beliefs, you will feel lighter. Life will not always be easy, and you will also become tempted to give in to the idea of perfectionism, but that is when you need to take a look at your journal and see all those things you have previously written as to why you love yourself.

Don't Hide Behind Excuses

If you want to build your self-esteem, you need to stop hiding behind excuses and refrain from partaking in the blame game. But if you don't do that, you will forever be framing yourself as the victim in all situations. You will also be dependent on others, and they say about you to feel validated. If you look towards external factors or other human beings to fulfill you, then you will never find happiness. Depending on someone will only breathe life into your codependent nature. In order to change your life, you need to stop making excuses and take responsibility for every action you take.

But yes, you also have to remember that you are not responsible for everything that happens in your life. Some things are only accidents or random acts of violence. Thinking that you are responsible for everything can be overwhelming. So, you need to judge whether you are responsible for something that is happening in your life or not. The first step towards living responsibly in building self-awareness. Having said this, most of you will see that to adopt this way of living, you have to undergo a 180-degree change, and this will not be easy. It will be a daunting task, but you don't have to do everything all at once. It should be a step-by-step process.

So, start by focusing on your behavior before blaming others for your feelings. Sit down in a quiet place and think about how you have contributed to your current position in life. You can maintain a journal too. Do you blame others when your plans are not executed the way you thought they would? But you need to start taking responsibility even if it was not you who directly caused what happened. Do you

58

make phony excuses whenever you are late to reach somewhere? Stop doing this and own up to your tardiness. You will see how changed you feel the moment you start taking responsibility.

Take Action

Only learning will never be enough. You have to put all that you have learned into action. Yes, you will have to take some risks in the process, but in the end, it will be all worth it. Set your boundaries or express yourself. Do something you haven't done before. You will definitely feel uncomfortable in the beginning, but that is okay.

Low self-esteem is often accompanied by shame, and that is what makes it even more difficult for you to take risks because you have a fear that others will be judging you. If you have had shaming adults in your life, then you must have faced difficulty in acknowledging your feelings, let alone express them. When you become an adult, your childhood experience of shame hinders you from taking action towards personal growth. You need to remember something. Your growth will be stagnated the moment you cow away from taking self-affirming actions. Your self-esteem will not be built in a day. There will be obstacles, and you have to be determined enough to overcome them all. You need to put yourself first and make the necessary decisions.

When you go to the gym after a long time or for the first time, you will find that your muscles feel sore. But if you want to continue going to the gym, you will have to fight that soreness anyway, and after a few days, it will go away. It is the same with your self-esteem. The moment you start taking some actions, there will be self-doubt or anxiety. But you still need to continue doing what you are doing, and you will no longer feel those shackles holding you down. The moment you start taking actions, you will have way lesser resentments, and your relationships will become less complex as well.

So, start making a list of things you have been piling up for quite some time and start doing them one by one. Don't wait for anyone else because it is your life, and it is you who has to challenge your fears.

Engage in Positive Self-Talk

Codependents have the habit of putting themselves down with negative thoughts. And that is why it is even more important for you to engage in positive self-talk. It is only you who can choose to be yourself, and it is also you who can decide to be against your own self. If you decide to be negative, then you will be sabotaging your own growth, as you must have noticed in the previous points that I have mentioned. So, planting the seeds of positivity is very crucial. If you are down or feeling low, it is your responsibility to live yourself up. You should not depend on any third person to do it for you.

Build your own mantra or positive dialogue that you can write down or reiterate whenever you are anxious, afraid, or sad. This dialogue should give you the courage to try something new and take risks. It should promote you to become more independent and courageous. If you believe you can, you will, but if you believe from the beginning that you cannot, then you will never be able to do it. Everyone likes a pat on the back and compliments for their hard work,

60

but do you have to depend on others for it? No, self-love teaches you to be your own friend and love yourself. You can acknowledge your hard work and compliment yourself. This will motivate you to work harder.

If you haven't noticed yet, then let me tell you something. The warmth that you get from the praise of others is not long-lasting, and it will quickly fade away. But when you give the same praise to yourself, it will linger longer. You can develop the habit of listing those things you love about yourself, no matter how small those things are. You can also list the things that you are grateful for because this will help you block all the negativity.

Stay Authentic

One of the most common problems that codependents face is that they are afraid to show their true selves to others, fearing that they will be humiliated. They have endured so much humiliation and loathing since their childhood days that now they have grown up to not accept themselves for the way they are. They fear that the moment people will know them for the way they are, they will be abandoned and left behind by those they hold dear. But you also have to understand that in order to overcome codependency, you have to live authentically.

So, in order to live authentically, you have to first trust and know yourself. You have to learn to express yourself and also be self-responsible. There should be no difference between the way you present yourself to others and the way you are in real life. It will be a challenge, but if you remain persistent, you will overcome it. Again, the first step is to write down all the discrepancies that you think exists between your real self and the person you portray yourself to be in front of the outside world. Then, think about how you would feel if you expressed your true self and spent your entire week just being you. Write down what you think would happen if you simply denied worrying about what others think of you.

You can also try your hand at writing a story about yourself, more like an imaginary day where you did what you wanted. In this prose, write about your feelings. This will help you understand the hidden wishes that have been buried long ago, and you will be able to realize what freedom meant. When you are authentic, your relationships become stronger. But, on the other hand, if you are keeping secrets from your partner, you are repeating the same mistakes of the family you grew up in. Breakaway from the fear of rejection and reveal your true self.

Practice Keeping the Commitments You Make to Yourself

Codependents always try to accommodate others, and in that process, they break all the commitments they make to themselves. For example, you might have planned something for yourself, but the moment someone else required you at the same time, you gave up your needs and catered to theirs. This is what you need to stop if you want to practice self-love. You need to make commitments for your own well-being, and you also have to learn to stick to those commitments. The moment you break the commitments, you need to remember that you are abandoning yourself.

Always think about your self-interest and then make the decisions in your life. You will be way happier if you lead your life in that way. Sometimes, things in your interest might not give you instant gratification, but they are good for the long run. You have to judge those pros and cons and then make your ultimate choice. Always aim at increasing your self-esteem. This will keep you healthy.

Another reason why you should not fail your own commitments is because it is a way of keeping up to your own expectations. But you also have to make sure that your expectations are not unrealistic. For example, you might be thinking about joining the gym for months but have not done it yet. Then it will be you who will get fed up with yourself one day, and then your inner critic will break your self-esteem even more. Sometimes, making the decision will be like standing at a crossroads. You will be confused about which decision will bring you more happiness. At that time, you have to listen to yourself and jot down legitimate reasons that crop up in your mind. You also have to stand up to your inner critic and stop it from haranguing you so that you can make your decision.

Practice Self-Love and Self-Compassion

The moment you raise your image in your own eyes, your self-esteem will start developing because it largely depends on self-evaluation. When you act contrary to what you think or what you want, it will subconsciously lower your levels of self-esteem. On the contrary, when you learn to accept yourself with no strings attached, you will come to a steady point in life. Start by catching yourself whenever you are comparing yourself to others or demeaning yourself in your

63

mind just because you think you are not enough. You need to stop right there and remind yourself that everyone is unique and everyone has their own flaws.

When you learn self-acceptance, you will feel lighter, and you will no longer be struggling to fit in. You will also learn to become authentic. Your inner self will start to reveal itself, and you can sit back and relax. Consequently, you also need to work on practicing self-forgiveness. If you do not learn to forgive yourself for your past actions, you will not be able to accept yourself fully. So, you can start by making a list of all those things you think you are guilty about. With each of these things, make a list of the motives you had and then judge the circumstances at the time you committed the act. You also need to judge why you thought that choice was the best at that time. You then need to analyze what the experience taught you, and in what way would you have handled it today.

Lastly, you need to understand the true meaning of self-love. Many confuse it with egoism, but it is not. The more you learn to love yourself, the better you will be able to love others in your life as well. Loving yourself or others means that you will learn to accept, respect, and understand. You need to practice compassion by caring and not for others but for yourself. You need to start seeing yourself in the same compassionate light as you see others. Loving yourself is not about doing good things for a day. It is more like a journey. It is a good start to do something for yourself, even if it involved ten minutes of your day. You can work yourself up from there and slowly give yourself more time.

Engage in Creative Expression

Develop some hobby or some sort of creative expression that you love because, at that time, you will be spending your time in something that is not your vocation. You will be enjoying the activity for its own sake and not because someone asked you to do it. It might be something very simple, like collecting stamps, and it can also be something like photography, dance, or music. Indulging in some sort of creative expression will help you to relax your mind and senses, and you will also be able to draw inspiration to lead your day-to-day life. These activities also act as a powerful channel for healing your soul. When you do something you love and not something for pleasing others, you don't care about perfectionism, and that is exactly what you need to overcome codependency. You need to give wings to your creativity, and this will give you joy. You will be enjoying the moment without worrying about others in your life.

You need to make yourself understand that it is okay to be messy. Doing something creative does not mean that you have to be the best at it. The idea is to have fun and enjoy yourself. You need not focus on the product but the journey. Think about this—was there some hobby in your childhood that you couldn't pursue or didn't have enough time to do? Then why not start today? Learn to play an instrument or take care of a pet. You can also try your hand at writing because writing about your feelings is a great way to heal your soul.

You need to understand that only you have the key to your happiness. So, find the activities that make you happy and pursue them. The moment you leave something untouched, you will bear the regret of not pursuing it. So, why carry that discontent when you can pursue your hobbies now? Even if it means doing something unprofitable, do it for the sake of your happiness. Don't let your thoughts or any external influence discourage you from pursuing something in life. Take a small step towards your goals every day, and one fine day, you will see you have reached a bit farther. Pay attention to all those things that stimulate your senses and make you feel happy and then plan your day accordingly with equal parts of everything.

Feel Good About Yourself

Now that you have taken so many steps towards recovery from your state of codependency, it is time that you feel a bit good about yourself. It is quite difficult to take up new things, but now that you have managed to do it, pat yourself on the back and praise yourself. Stop focusing your energy on your old thoughts and spend more time with your new self. Just like the seedlings need sunshine and water to grow, you need positivity and love. Surround yourself with people who help you stay on track and cut off those people who reinforce your old negative thoughts.

You need to be around those who share your vibe; otherwise, they are going to bring you down. Don't let the small obstacles in your path throw you off your track. You have made some progress, and you need to stick to that. Hard times are temporary, and they are eventually going to go away if you are persistent towards your ultimate goal. Learn to direct all your strength towards a positive goal, and nothing can stop you from achieving what you want. Create a strategy that you can follow and refrain from all those things which bring back negativity or make you feel bad.

But yes, don't go into denial about things that need your attention.

Whether or not you change into a positive person is totally up to you, but these are some of the things that you can do. Most of the things that you do in a day are a part of your routine. But what you need to do is interrupt that same routine and include newer things. This will give you greater opportunities in life. Everything related to self-love is about stopping those routine behaviors that are toxic or causing you to become negative.

You need to control your habits of procrastination and get going. Anything that is self-defeating should be nipped in the bud. Most people shy away from practicing self-love because they correlate it to being selfish. Most children grow up without knowing anything about the concept of self-love or self-compassion and so learning it will take time. Self-love will teach you how you can depend only on yourself and not on others for love and appraisal. This is a direct contrast to everything that codependency is about, and thus practicing self-love is a very good strategy to curb your habits of codependency.

Also, if you do not love yourself, you will never be able to take compliments from others. Has it ever happened to you that you couldn't bask in the compliment someone gave you just because you thought you don't deserve it? If yes, then the solution to this is also that same thing—self-love. If you don't love yourself the way you are, your natural inclination to most compliments will be that you don't deserve them.

Chapter 6:

Steps to Conquer Your Freedom by Learning to Let Go

One of the main characteristics of codependents is that they are overly attached to everything in their life. This is because codependents always need someone to be there for them. All the attachments they form in their life is out of need. They need others to behave in a certain way so that they can feel normal and okay. But in this chapter, you will learn how you can let go of your unhealthy ways and prevent yourself from becoming over-involved with anything in life.

Understanding Nonattachment and Over-Involvement

When you get attached to your family members of very close people in your life, it is completely normal. But the pattern followed by codependents is not healthy and often results in problems and pain. They tend to become over-involved very easily. The solution to this problem is nonattachment. This means you have to learn the art of neutrality and how you can practice it to gradually withdraw yourself not only physically but also emotionally from those things which are holding you back.

Are you not sure whether you are over-involved or not? Well, to put it simply, you are over-involved when you do not have proper boundaries, and everything in between is blurred. This is mostly when your mood depends on others and not on yourself. You will also react strongly to every comment or judgment passed by others. With over-involvement, you will ponder about the thoughts and feelings of others and become quite obsessed with it. You will also try to give in to people-pleasing out of fear of abandonment and rejection. You also become myopic the moment you become over-involved with someone or something.

Others gradually become an extension of yourself and vice-versa. You try to get a hold over everything so that you can feel okay. You try to keep them pleased and impress them in any way possible. But when they feel suffocated with your constant presence and demand some personal space for themselves, you show anger and resentment. All of this shows that you are definitely over-involved with that particular person.

But, on the other hand, if you know how to become nonattached, then you will be encouraging others and be compassionate to them rather than being clingy. You will be authentic and not manipulate others to stay in peace. You will know to respect others and their thoughts and not always try to persuade others into your own opinion. You will also honor their wish of having space, and you will also enjoy your own company. Thus, in short, you will have appropriate boundaries, and you will know how to accept reality.

Thus, nonattachment is about setting free from the toxic glue that keeps you bonded in a codependent relationship. You will learn to let go of the problems faced by other people and their expectations. You will simply mind your own business and not worry about what others are saying or reacting to. But all of this doesn't mean that you will be neglecting your duties. There is no relationship between nonattachment and physical proximity. Also, nonattachment is not the same as being emotionally isolated. You do not need to turn your feelings off to be nonattached. You simply need to strike a balance between your needs and others'.

Learn to Let Go

There are profound and endless benefits to letting go of certain things in life. This is not only important for your personal growth but also for maintaining healthy relationships in your personal life. This, in turn, will help in maintaining a feeling of inner peace. Here are some of the benefits of letting go—

You Learn How to Love

If you want to shower someone with unconditional love, you first have to become nonattached and let go of any resentments or grudges. But being nonattached in a relationship might seem paradoxical to you now. But in the case of relationships, being nonattached means that you are giving your partner enough space to grow and take care of their own needs.

Letting go is more like focusing on the bigger picture by taking one step back. You need to understand that you are your partner are two completely different human beings, and thus you both have diverging needs. Your perspectives and life experiences are different, as well.

But this understanding will dawn upon you with time. But when you understand the separateness that you have with your partner, you will understand the true meaning of non-attachment as well. Remember that seeing someone for the unique person they are means that you are honoring them and giving them both and love and space.

You Will Be at Peace With Yourself

Whenever you are trying to gain control over someone else, it means that a person already has control over you, maybe not directly or physically, but emotionally.

That is why having control over that person or getting the upper hand becomes so important to you. But when you stop judging, managing or helping others, you will not have anything to worry about. You do not have to hold yourself responsible for the mistakes and problems of other people. You are allowed to do whatever it is that you want to do, and you will be free.

When you take a step further and learn to become nonattached from the moods and comments of others, you gain power. You become determined to mind your own business instead of reacting to the pettiest things in life. You take the upper hand over your own thoughts and choose how you will be reacting or behaving in each situation. This boosts your self-esteem in an instant. Thus, you will no longer be on a rollercoaster ride, and your mind will finally be at peace.

You Will Have More Time for Your Own Needs

The moment you let go of others' needs, you will have more time in your hands to cater to your own needs. You will no longer be consumed by spending time with others or being responsible for the acts of others. You will be finally living a life for your own self instead of someone else. Thus, you will be able to focus on your hobbies, interests, and career.

You Learn What Independence Is

With nonattachment, your life is in your own hands, and you learn to become independent and also responsible. The person you had been controlling all this time also has to take his/her own responsibility, and thus, they get a chance to recognize their mistakes and learn from them. Thus, nonattachment brings benefits to both parties, and both of them understand the true meaning of independence.

What is Self-Responsibility?

It is quite natural when you feel sad about the problems of your loved ones, but it is not okay to feel responsible for the same even when you had nothing to do with it. Codependents always try to resolve others' problems in an attempt to lessen their suffering. But you need to understand something as a codependent, and that is—you can only fix that part of a relationship, which is about you. You are responsible only for your actions and thoughts, and so you cannot do anything about what happens to others.

You can definitely cheer someone up in their hour of need, and there is nothing wrong in doing that. Codependency is when you take it upon yourself to make the other person happy by sacrificing your own needs. Codependents also have the habit of taking extreme measures to accommodate others in a relationship, and they become people pretzels. Make a list of all those things you think you are responsible for then judge them based on whether you are truly responsible for them or you are simply doing it to make someone happy.

Stop Helping Too Much

Sometimes codependents end up helping others way too much even when the other person didn't ask for any help. If you are doing this, then you must remember that you are violating the boundaries of that person as well. That person might not want you interfering with certain aspects of his/her life, but you are doing it anyway just because it fills the void inside of you. You cannot try to manage a person's life at all times because that is disrespecting on so many levels. It even communicates a message that the person is not strong or competent enough to look after his/her own needs.

When it comes to reality, it is not your duty to decide what is good for someone else because it completely relies on the desires and expectations of that particular individual and not you. When you try to change or control that person, you are affecting their self-esteem. What you can do is be sympathetic or be a good listener. But you should not impose your decisions upon them. You can play the role of a trusted friend and advisor but never become so much entangled in their life that you end up making their choices for them.

What Should You Do If Someone Asks for Help?

Having already discussed how you should not help someone too much, you must be wondering what you should do in case someone asks for help. Well, this can be quite a tricky situation and depends on a lot of things. The first thought that might come to your mind is that you are not violating any boundaries when you are being asked to help. But everything is not so black and white, as you will understand after completing this section.

Suppose your friend asked you to help him out, and you assisted him in making some decisions. In doing that, you are interfering with his own problem-solving abilities. If you make his decisions for him, you are taking away his opportunity to find strength. Also, once you start helping the person, you might not be able to stop yourself from helping him over and over again due to your codependent nature, and soon, it will go on like a cycle.

So, what would be a better idea? You can listen to the problems of your friend and then you can ask him to produce his ideas on dealing with the matter. You can give him support and encouragement to proceed with his idea of dealing with the situation.

Keep a Check on Your Expectations

Expectations can bring a lot of pain if not kept under control. One of the main problems in every relationship is having unrealistic expectations. You might want your spouse to behave in a certain way, but when they don't, you feel disappointed. That is when the seed of resentment is planted in a relationship. These feelings can spread like wildfire and destroy the entire relationship.

You might even develop some preconceived notions about how your relationship should be rather than enjoying it how it is. You might have these imaginations perhaps from the way you saw your parents' marriage or some superficial marriage on a TV show. This creates expectations that you want your spouse to fulfill. To you, your expectations might seem natural, but to your spouse, they can be unrealistic and unattainable. So, even if you have certain expectations, you need to judge whether the other person is also willing to fulfill those expectations.

You need to judge your relationship objectively. You cannot simply go one expecting things from your spouse without doing anything yourself. As yourself whether you have always been vocal about what you want. You should not expect your spouse or anyone, for that matter, to read your mind and magically know what you want. If you want something to happen in a particular way, you have to say it. Also, if you have already asked someone to do something repeatedly but that person has not yet done it, then you should not be manipulating that person into doing what you want. If you have the habit of wanting others to read your mind, then you need to break free from this habit. The first step is to acknowledge the things you want and then gathering up the courage to ask for them.

Stop Overreacting

Codependents easily react to other people's comments and actions. It is easy to do that, and your thoughts become centered around what others are thinking about you. That is how overreactions are born. You need to ask yourself and answer the question truly that for how long are you upset. If you have been upset for long, it means that you have been accumulating all that anger and frustration, and thus it is now being poured out all at once. You also need to judge whether the thing that triggered you was reasonable enough or not.

On the other hand, some codependents have the habit of exaggerating almost everything in their life. They jump to conclusions without thinking about anything. You make mountains out of molehills, and you feel as if you are always compelled to react or show some action to everything that comes your way. When you blame others, you are actually covering up your own shame and guilt. How you are reacting is not about others but about your own personality and also the experience you had in your past.

You need to stop reacting and communicate your thoughts in a better way. You need to learn to tolerate the different opinions shown by others. It is easy to become intoxicated by anger and react harshly, but you should restrain yourself from doing so. You need to ask yourself whether your reactions are helping the situation in any manner. Most of the time, the answer will be no, and so you need to think of other ways in which you can handle the situation.

Accept the Reality

Learning to accept is a major part of letting go. It does not happen in a day, but step by step, you can achieve it. Awareness is the first step towards change. But you should not confuse acceptance with approval. Acceptance is simply acknowledging the fact that something exists. It means you are taking charge of your life and your responsibilities. It also doesn't mean that you are going to accept any abuse happening towards you. It is basically an empowering step after which you can decide what you can do about your present situation.

There are different levels of acceptance. You also need to come to terms with the fact that you are sometimes powerless over certain situations in life. You also need to accept that it is you who has to take action and change things. The moment you let go of your unrealistic expectations and accept the reality for what it is, you will feel the burden lift off your shoulders. When you accept things, you are also able to set new boundaries or even seek help from others. You will be able to calm down your inner turmoil and understand that everything in life is not meant to be controlled.

Chapter 7:

Speak Up and Break Through Dysfunctional Communication

Effective communication is the key to the well-being of every relationship. It also reflects your level of self-esteem. But in the case of codependents, communication is not so easy and often dysfunctional. This is because while growing up, no one in their family communicated openly with them and so they never learned it. When they are born in dysfunctional families, usually one or both of the parents are abusive or aggressive, and that is what they learn to be. But there are others who will isolate themselves and tune out of normal day-to-day life. In both cases, there will be disharmony, and their future relationships will not be healthy.

If you have already read all the previous chapters, then by now, you have started to understand what your feelings and thoughts are and how you can refrain from controlling every situation. And with proper practice, you will learn the means of effective communication as well. When your focus is based on someone else, you react differently, always keeping in mind how that other person will react. But, when you convey your feelings without any aim of manipulation, that is when the reaction of others becomes less and less important to you.

78

It is not only your words that make up an effective communication strategy. It involved your entire body. You need to have proper expressions and also maintain eye contact with the person you are talking to. Your posture and muscular tension also matter. Additionally, your voice will determine your confidence, and thus various aspects of your voice like your tone, volume, emphasis, cadence, and enunciation is of crucial importance.

Be Assertive

If you want to inspire influence and project confidence, then you need to practice assertive communication. If you do not know how to do it, then don't worry as it is no rocket science and can be learned. All you need to do is be patient with yourself. But first, you need to understand the meaning of being assertive.

Assertiveness is all about stating your true feelings and emotions in a polite yet clear way. You can also include explanations as to why you feel the way you feel. The main qualities of assertive communication are that it is honest, direct, and open, and nothing like being rude or aggressive or selfish. If you are willing to engage in assertive communication, then you have to be honest about your feelings. Your words that come out of your mouth should match will your feelings. Codependents are usually different on the outside than they are on the inside, and this is something you need to eliminate. For example, your body language will reveal how you are truly feeling, even if you say that you are fine. If you are in an intimate relationship with someone, eye contact is mandatory.

The purpose of assertive communication is to express yourself in a polite manner and not to vent out. The moment you fail to maintain a level of courtesy, you will lose your listeners. Your criticism should be constructive, and you have to treat your listener with respect. You also need to be concise about what you are saying. Stop beating around the bush and come to the point. The moment you are being wordy, your listener will know that you are not aware of what you want. Codependents have this habit of being indirect. But you need to practice directness and not make any camouflaged comments. Stop speaking abstractly or with hints and also stop making assumptions.

Also, communication is a two-way approach. You need to listen to what the person in front of you has to say if you truly want him/her to listen to you. People will be more receptive to you the moment they understand that they matter to them, and you can bring about this feeling by listening and engaging with them.

Express Your Feelings and Needs

Your feelings and your thoughts are two different things, and you should not be confused between the two during communication. For example, if someone stood you up on a date, and you call that person to tell them how inconsiderate they were, you are not communicating your feelings. You are simply telling them what you think. This is wrong. Instead of focusing on their faults, focus on what you felt, and convey it. Tell them how important that date was to you and that you felt sad because the person stood you up. Claim your feelings, and half your problems will be solved.

The moment you claim your feelings, you will see that you do not need to justify yourself for anything. In some cases, you will see that the only initial feelings that crop up are those of anger and resentment, but with each passing moment, you have to learn to dig deep and understand the deeper thoughts. The process becomes difficult when you are too emotional. The point is to communicate how you felt rather than venting your anger on the person in front of you.

Codependents usually do not focus on their own needs. They fear humiliation and rejection, and all of this arises from the shaming they faced in their childhood years. If you have already pinpointed your needs, then the best way to express them is to directly ask for them to be fulfilled. But in doing so, you should not be criticizing someone else or end up blaming them. That is the wrong approach. You have to instead tell the person about the positive effects of fulfilling your needs. You can also tell them how you feel when your needs are not met. This can seem frightening as you are making yourself vulnerable, but this will also make your relationship stronger and bring you closer to your loved ones.

Learn to Take a Stand

You need to take some direct positions in your life if you want to practice assertive communication. This means you have to make clear statements about what you want to do and what you don't want to do. You need to be vocal about your likes and dislikes. But, as already mentioned before, codependents have an indirect approach to everything in their life. They always try to avoid conflicts by concealing their true selves and avoiding situations where they have to ask questions. But not taking a stand means you are leaving every feeling unresolved.

Also, taking a stand does not mean you have to react to situations, and this is exactly what codependents do. They overreact, giving rise to conflicts, and then they shut themselves off from further conversations fearing that the same conflict would arise again. This goes on and on like a cycle.

Then there are some people who think there is no use taking a position or expressing their opinions because no one would care. But you need to understand that you are not speaking up for others. You are speaking up for yourself, and so it doesn't matter what other people's opinions are. The moment you speak up, you will start feeling better about yourself because, finally, you will have expressed what you truly feel.

Beware of Pitfalls

Some pitfalls might arise in your path, and they are specially meant to keep the codependents away from confrontations. Some of the things that you need to do to overcome obstacles are as follows:

- **Stop victimizing yourself**—Codependents are often used to portraying themselves as the victim. But you should be taking responsibility for your actions and describe what you are feeling rather than victimizing yourself.

- **Don't generalize**—If you start making generalized statements instead of making being specific, the conversation will become more about whose memory serves best. For example, you might be telling your spouse that he never remembers your anniversary, but what you actually meant to say was that he has stopped paying heed to your happiness.

- **Don't throw empty apologies**—If you are apologizing, then mean it. Empty apologies can be really annoying. If you are not sure whether you owe someone an apology or not, then it always better to clarify the situations instead of saying sorry without meaning it.

- **Stop justifying yourself**—When you try to explain yourself at every point, you simply give others the opportunity to criticize you or judge you. It also shows that you have a low level of self-esteem. It gives the person in front of you a chance to continue the argument. It is reason enough that you want something, and you don't need to justify your wishes. You can also change your mind any time you want, and you don't need to give anyone an explanation for that.

- **Stick to the subject**—In order to avoid confrontations, codependents have the habit of changing the subject of conversations. But you need to learn to respond directly to everything without changing the subject.

- **Avoid the blame game**—As I have already mentioned this a lot of times before, I am not going into the details, but you will be tempted to blame others for your actions. You simply have to control your urge to do that.

Set Limits and Boundaries

We have discussed the effects of dysfunctional boundaries in previous chapters, and here, we are going to discuss how setting boundaries is a prerequisite for effective communication. When you set boundaries, you refrain from situations where others can take advantage of your goodness. You will be able to protect yourself. Boundaries don't have to be complex. It can be something as simple as spending lesser hours on your phone or something like not spending time with a toxic person.

When you set boundaries, you are honoring your own needs and wished over that of others. You are standing up for yourself, and that is something that will help you in the long run. When you say no to others, it means that you are saying yes to your own needs. You will gain a sense of freedom. You can also resist answering questions hurled at you because you are not obliged to have an answer to everything. You should take your time while you are setting boundaries and think it through. You need to be clear about what you want; otherwise, your boundaries will get messed up.

If you are not ready to set boundaries, but you do so anyway, you will be undermining your own credibility.

Confront Abuse

Abuse should always be confronted. If you keep on enduring the abuse done to you, it will give your abuser all the more reason to continue the emotional manipulation because he/she knows that you are not going to leave. In order to start the confrontation, you first have to identify the situations when you are emotionally abused. You need to identify the tactics that the abuser is using and maintain a note of them. Identify your feelings when you are being abused. Then you need to instill self-respect and a belief that you deserve better and that you deserve to be respected.

Set limits and practice saying no to the things you don't want to do or the things that make you feel bad. Work on raising your self-esteem because enduring abuse has a lot to do with low self-esteem. Most of the time, people stay in an abusive relationship because they have given up all hope, and they think that abuse is what they deserve. Make firm and direct statements with the abuser and state your feelings directly. The moment you start setting boundaries and make strong statements, the abuser will get the message and know that you are not going to be affected by the abuse anymore, and thus, the abuse will eventually stop.

Confronting the abuse might not make your relationship better because there are deeper issues that need to be resolved. But it will definitely help to build your self-confidence, and you will learn some important life skills.

Chapter 8:

10 Ways to Love Yourself

The best way to overcome codependency is to love yourself and give yourself priority, and I'm sure you must have understood this by now. But if you are pondering over how you are going to do that, then I have listed 10 easy ways of loving yourself, and remember, it is not selfish to put yourself first. Selfishness is when you lack something and desire what others have. But love comes out of a good feeling, and you enjoy staying in the presence of others without thinking or wanting to change them in any way.

Follow Your Passions

One of the best ways to love yourself is by following your passions. You need to understand that the keys to your happiness are in your hands alone. You will be filled with regret and discontent the moment you decide to forego your passions or help someone else by not prioritizing your needs. You do not need to cross oceans. A small step every day towards what you love is enough to make you feel happy and content. If you are still not sure about what your passion is, then you can try and think about all those things that stimulate you.

Also, when you choose to follow your passion, your life will be filled with a sense of purpose that you did not have before. And this purpose will be centered around your own happiness and not to please someone else. Gradually, when you see that your dreams are now becoming to reality, you will gain self-confidence, and your self-esteem will start growing too. Set micro-goals towards your ultimate goal, and the moment you achieve a micro goal, celebrate that success and give a pat on your back for your victory towards recovery.

Compliment Yourself

Compliments bring enthusiasm and encouragement, but should you depend on someone else for these compliments? The answer is no. You should be your own positive support. Appreciate yourself and repeat the compliments over and over again. Don't take yourself for granted because if you do, others will do the same. Notice that good in yourself, acknowledge them, and compliment them. The moment you hear the encouragement from yourself, you will feel good and energized. But you also have to remove every ounce of self-doubt from your body and pay heed to even the smallest achievements you make.

All of this is very much correlated. Positive encouragement leads to positive action. This is because if you hear compliments, you will be motivated to work better and take actions that fetch better results for your own well-being. This, in turn, will increase your levels of confidence, and you will continue cheering yourself forward, and the cycle of positivity will go on and on. Wake up every morning and compliment yourself for even the simplest things, and you will never feel alone or need anyone to complete you.

Choose Your Friends Carefully

Now you must be wondering what your friends have to do with you loving yourself. Well, there is a direct connection, even though it is not visible. Your friends have a huge impact on the quality of your life. Your friends can not only affect your mental health, but also your physical well-being. If the social circle you stay in always spreads negativity or hurls hurtful words at you, then you should leave them at once. Your mind will constantly be in pain if you are with such a group of people. Even if it is only one person who is insulting, you should distance yourself away from him/her.

On the other hand, if you are surrounded by people who love you from the bottom of their hearts, you will feel good about yourself too. They will shower you with their kind words and make you feel positive.

Supportive relationships can help codependents break away from their dependency. So, now you see why I said you should choose your friends carefully? Your social circle is of crucial importance to your personality, and anything of that importance should be dealt with care, isn't it?

Learn to Forgive Yourself for Your Self-Perceived Mistakes

Loving yourself has some barriers that you need to overcome, and one of the most common ones is forgiving yourself for the things that you have done in the past. It can be anything. Sometimes you might be feeling bad about how you treated your ex a couple of years back. Or it can be something that you did in school, which you now think was unjust. If you resonate with this feeling and if you have such painful memories that keep cropping up in your mind, then you need to forgive yourself. Self-forgiveness paves the path to self-love.

You have to remind yourself that you did what you could have done at that time. You might not have had the maturity to understand that what you were doing could hurt someone else. But what is important is that you realize it now and you know that you are not going to repeat your mistake. Forgiving yourself might not be easy, and it will entirely depend upon the emotional wound that you have. If the wound is too deep, forgiveness will take time.

Spend Time With Yourself

As a codependent person, it is in your nature to give all your time to others and not keep anything for yourself. But you will have to change that behavior if you want to love yourself. You might be learning to love others, but you will never be happy if you do not know how to love yourself. So, focus on cultivating a positive relationship with yourself. For this, you need to set aside some time to spend alone reflecting on things you love. Regardless of whether you are an extrovert or introvert, some time alone doing things you love will benefit you in several ways.

You can also go on dates with yourself. There is nothing wrong about treating yourself to a nice restaurant or taking yourself out to a movie. In fact, doing these things will allow you to do everything the way you love to do. You do not have to depend on anyone else for their approval or make any compromises. It will be a day where everything will be according to what you love. You will be amazed at what a great impact such alone time can make on your life.

Meditate

Meditation helps in self-acceptance and thus helps you love yourself for the way you are. All those circling thoughts in your mind that belittle you or make you think that you are not enough will go away if you practice meditation and mindfulness daily. You will wake up every morning feeling happier and more energized. Meditation is considered to be a very strong mental practice because it helps in rewiring your brain in a way that does not allow any negative thoughts to seep in.

When you meditate, you stop judging your emotions and feelings and start observing them. You can come out of your cocoon of shame and finally accept your feelings with open arms. You will also become full of positive emotions that will fill your body with energy. Meditation also helps you to deal with anxiety, which is a common trait in codependents.

Have Enough Sleep

If you want to be happy, you also need to have a well-rested brain, and so you need to sleep properly. Prepare a proper routine and stick to it. Even research has shown that sleep is directly related to the overall happiness of a human being. Your tendency to become depressed increases by many folds whenever you are sleep deprived. This is because when you lack sleep, your stress hormones begin increasing. Sleep deprivation also leads to gain of weight and several other health problems. When you are well-rested, you are more patient while talking and communicating with others. This eliminates the chances of misunderstandings.

Without good sleep, people tend to yell even in the pettiest situations. Sleep affects your work performance, which, in turn, leads to dissatisfaction at the workplace. You crash out soon, and you cannot handle the workload given to you while you watch your fellow employees do better and get faster promotions. The moment you sleep well, you can get rid of all these problems and also fight anxiety. You will not be fatigued easily and thus complete all your tasks on time. This will make you happy and content.

Work on Self-Trust

The more self-reliant you are, the happier you will be. Do you expect others to do things for you? Do you easily get affected by what other people think of you? Do you always expect people to be there for you? In the case of codependents, most of the answers will be yes. That is how codependents are. But when you start trusting yourself and build your own identity, you do not have to depend on others.

When you give up on self-trust, you will become needier, and you will give toxic people the opportunity to shatter you and manipulate you. You need to have your own voice. Don't shy away from situations of confrontation.

Don't run away from setbacks. Treat them as a learning opportunity because that is what they are. The way you behave in the face of adversity will determine a lot of things about your character. If you lose your courage in times of need, you will grow to hate yourself for it.

Your self-image will become lowered in your own eyes, and this will bring discontent. But if you increase your self-trust, you will live without any regrets holding you back.

Be Grateful

How often do you practice gratitude? Are you thankful for the things you have in life? Do you thank the universe every morning because of the basic necessities of life? If not, then you should start doing these things because of one simple reason—they will bring you happiness. When you are grateful, you will be focusing on the good things in life and also the good qualities of your own self. You will see that you are not that bad you imagine yourself to be. This will bring about self-love.

Being generous and considering everyone's point of view before responding will make you a better person. This will bring happiness from within, and you will love yourself. This will also help you in dealing with the frustrations of life.

Stop Trying to Be Perfect

Perfectionism kills self-love. No one is perfect, and everyone makes mistakes at some point or the other. Life is not a 'do or die' situation where you have to be perfect or fail. There is a middle ground, and that is what life is about. When you try to lead a life free of mistakes, you are always tensed and loathe yourself for the simplest things. You become too hard on yourself, and in this way, you will never be able to enjoy the true essence of life. Things might not always go as planned, but it is alright. Sometimes, you end up learning a lot of things when things don't go as planned.

Perfectionism also compels you to constantly compare yourself with others. This brings about a competition that you have to live up to the expectations that others have set for you. But if you start leading your life for yourself and not for others, you will realize that everyone is unique, and you

92

are too. So, try to be the best version of yourself and not better than someone else. When you think everything is not perfect, you cannot be happy. But if you take a step back and look at your life from a third-person point of view, you will see that you have a lot of things that others don't. In short, your life is perfect for someone else. So, do you see that perfectionism is nothing but an illusion? Don't fall prey to it and be your true self. Give your best in everything that you do, but don't compare your efforts to that of others.

Chapter 9:

Embrace Yourself and Stop Depending on Others

Emotional dependency is the core sign of codependency, as you have learned right at the beginning of this book. This dependency can be toxic because you leave yourself entirely in the hands of someone else, and this is also a vital thing to address. Overcoming this sense of dependency can be challenging and can be done only when you learn to embrace your true self. It takes not only practice but also patience. So, if you are determined to overcome unhealthy codependent situations and learn to embrace yourself, then here are some tips that you must keep in mind.

Don't Give Away Your Responsibility

Codependents are not confident enough to look after their own emotional needs, and thus, they mostly rely on others in this matter. They always reach out to others so that their needs can be met. But you have to remember that no matter how happy that other person makes you feel, you should not be running away from your own responsibilities. The moment you start relying on others for the basic tasks of life, you will be losing your confidence in your own self. The first step to developing your sense of responsibility is self-observation. You need to pinpoint those situations where your first instinct is to depend on someone else rather than solve the problem yourself.

For example, if you are lonely, you can either choose to summon someone to spend time with you, or you can do the things you love and keep yourself happy and satisfied. Taking responsibility is also hidden in the simple tasks of life. For example, if you have said something hurtful to your girlfriend, don't ask her best friend to go and talk to her. It is you who have said something to hurt her, and thus, it has to be you who will go and apologize. Being responsible also means making your own decisions. No matter how hard the process of making the decision is, commit to it and don't give in to the comfort of others, making the decisions for you. This is because you might not be agreeing with what others have decided for you, and this leads to conflicts.

Finally, I would also mention the fact that some people doubt their ability to make decisions because they think they are not good enough for it. This thought arises from the fact that codependents have the habit of constantly comparing themselves with others. You have to look inwards into your soul and stop judging yourself. Practice acceptance, and you will automatically become responsible for your actions.

Be There for Yourself

Codependents have the innate nature of instantly connecting with others and making time anyhow to be there for others in their time of need. But they seldom do the same for themselves as well. You need to become your own best friend and develop a good relationship with yourself. It is good to take care of others, but it is not good to shut the door on your needs. You need to maintain a balance between catering to others and to yourself. You need to work on releasing self-neglect. For this, the first step is to remind yourself every day that you are worthy, just like every other human being on this planet. You need to recognize what are your needs and feelings, and then you have to learn to prioritize your feelings over others.

Even if you are amidst a busy routine, you need to take some time out for your needs and deal with them strategically. Savor the time that you save for yourself, and you can even try your hand at new things every day. Embrace discovery, learning, and curiosity. You can also do some exercise every morning so that you can feel healthy. Sometimes people neglect themselves out of self-loathing because they think they are imperfect. Well, as I have said it multiple times before, everyone is imperfect, and you need to embrace your imperfections too. There are so many things that you can do to be there for yourself, and you might not be able to do them all at once. But it doesn't matter. Even if you ensure one thing at a time, you will notice gradual changes that will make you feel better. Self-development is a time-consuming process. Look after yourself by doing things that make you happy or feel better. Once you figure out something easy and yet refreshing, repeat it every day. It is important that you are consistent at taking care of yourself. You cannot expect development if you are indulging in self-love today, but tomorrow you go back to self-loathing.

Know Your Vulnerabilities

If you want to stop depending on others, then you need to know your vulnerabilities too. The moment you push away the feelings and thoughts in your mind, a void will start forming, and you will lose the connection to your soul over time. If you want to fill the void within yourself, then you should try things like journaling. But if you think you do not have enough time for that, you can even try to record voice messages, and they will serve as an audible journal. Self-expression is the best way to know yourself, and it is highly authentic too.

You depend on others primarily because you want someone to listen to what you have to say, and then you expect that person to support you. This comes from a place in your mind where you have given up on supporting yourself, and so you rely on outside influences. The moment you cow away from expressing yourself, you are bound to feel helpless. But when you explain your desires, feelings, hurt, frustrations, needs, and even shame, you will be aware of the feelings going on inside you. You will be seeing yourself in light of self-compassion.

You need to expose your vulnerabilities to yourself. This is because the only way in which you unlock your sense of self-compassion is by allowing yourself to feel what you are truly going through. This will also accompany a feeling of emotional release, and it is completely normal for that to happen because it can bring about healing. Are you feeling numbed by your emotions and thus cannot differentiate one feeling from the other? Then you should maintain a journal where you can write down all the deepest thoughts of your heart and go through it from time to time. This can do wonders in the process of embracing yourself, and with time, you will understand that there is nothing more beautiful than being comfortable with who you are.

Engage in Self-Parenting

Have you ever thought about the fact that how you would be treating yourself if you were someone else? It is in the basic instinct of everyone and especially codependents to love someone they hold dear. But when it comes to ourselves, we often back off from showering us with love. Some people are even unaware of this situation and do not realize how harshly they treat themselves. Codependents who have endured a traumatic childhood often fret about the fact that they were exposed to such things that a child should never endure. But they end up treating themselves in the same neglectful way as their parents. But you need to take the responsibility of your care into your own hands and consciously choose to be the parent to yourself you wished you had in childhood. You need to consciously choose self-care over self-harm every day. You need to be that like those supportive and good parents you always wanted. You should take your side even when no one does and console yourself on the rainy days. Be the big brother you never had or the best friend who can make everything better. Be all of this to yourself because you deserve it. You need to realize that you matter and stop discrediting your feelings.

In the beginning, you might be confused about where to start. But, well, the first thing you must ensure is to stop mistreating yourself. Catch yourself in the act and then change your behavior. You will have some part of your inner self telling you that you do not deserve all that bad behavior, and so, you have to hold on to that part of yourself and bathe yourself in kindness. Even the smallest degree of self-care and self-parenting can make you a whole lot better and relaxed.

In the previous point, we had discussed expressing your vulnerabilities to yourself. So, when you do that, there will be a certain amount of helplessness in the air. You need to take that opportunity and act as your own parent. Nurture your inner child and make your soul feel safe. You can even practice visualization and see yourself as a child and how you always wanted yourself to be treated. At times, you will not know what to do, and that this when you need to reassure yourself that you will eventually figure it all out.

Let Go of Attachments

Dependability begets attachments because the moment you depend on a person, you also become attached to them. The same applies to any object. There will be a strong desire for engagement whenever you are in a dependable relationship with someone or something. And the solution to this problem is breaking free from the attachment and staying in the present. There will be so many mental attachments that will hold you back. This is mostly the case when you are obsessed with something in your life.

So, if you want to let go of that dependability, you need to give yourself a break and also change your focus. Give all your focus on something and probably something that makes you happy. This will make you realize that you do not necessarily have to depend on one person or thing to fulfill your happiness. Deep breathing in a quiet place often helps to let go of attachments and free your mind.

Step Away from Emotional Cruelty

Do you always treat yourself harshly or criticize yourself without any apparent reason? Codependents usually use self-criticism as a form of coping mechanism that helps

99

them get through extreme circumstances, but this habit is not at all healthy. It is like self-abuse. You gradually become an emotional sadist to yourself. When there is no presence of compassion in your life, you use this emotional sadism as a form of an escape route. But you need to overcome the practice if you want to embrace yourself and feel happy.

You need to understand that your inner soul is a child and that it is purely innocent. You do not have to inflict any harsh punishments on it and maybe treat your soul with care in order to get the results you wanted. Putting yourself through habitual punishments will only destabilize your mental health, pushing you off the edge. But it will not happen in a day. Just think about it. You have been punishing yourself for years, and so if you want to heal, you will need to show self-support for a considerable period of time to grow and heal.

So, if you want to start taking responsibility for all the harsh things you say to yourself, then begin by making a list of harsh things that are currently on your mind. Then sit and ask yourself whether all of these things are actually true or simply an escape route to vent your anger and frustration on yourself. When you realize that you are not being fair, ask yourself what you would have done if it was someone you love in your place. Then, think about a better response that does not involve any harshness.

You need to keep an eye out for any suppressive reactions or thoughts that you are having because they can be highly toxic. Codependents are used to punishing themselves because they see their own selves in a negative light. But you should be encouraging yourself to be you and embrace all your qualities without judgment. You need to understand that the part of yourself that struggles the most is the part that needs the maximum amount of love that needs to be understood and not looked down upon.

Don't Think of Your Needs to Be Someone Else's Responsibility

You need to be able to mix freely with other people to embrace yourself. If you hold secret grudges against other people, then your behavior towards them will take the hit. Yes, it will be tempting to show your anger, but you need to hold back those thoughts and think about forgiveness. If someone is not present for you in a time of crisis, is it really justified to be angry with them?

After all, it is not their duty to be there for you. You must be the cornerstone of yourself.

Consider this. You might pass several homeless people in a day. Do you give every one of them something or even a small change? No, right? It is because you cannot do something for everyone in this world. Similarly, don't be an emotional beggar to others. It might sound harsh, but it is the truth. No one really has anything to owe to you. There are certain natural limitations to every relationship, and you simply have to accept this hard truth.

If you think that others 'must' or 'should' help you in a particular situation, then that is where you are going wrong, and you are letting your codependent personality get the better of you. So, stop pestering others to help you when they clearly don't want to. Give others the free will to come and go as they please because it is not their responsibility to babysit you.

Eliminate All Self-Destructive Patterns

As already mentioned at the beginning of this book, your childhood plays a big role in shaping you or even making you a codependent person in the first place. If you were not attended to in your adolescence or childhood years, then you will become needy when you grow up. So, sit down and think about the events that traumatized you when you were younger because this will help you figure out the root cause of your problems. You will come to know where your emotional dependency stems from. Now, you need to understand that your future does not necessarily have to be like your past.

But yes, exploring past events doesn't mean that you have to get lost in them. You have to do it only to the extent to which you can let go of certain toxic thought patterns. You had formed these patterns in childhood because, at that time, you had no idea why was all that happening to you. Stop reliving the same trauma over and over again by facing it once and for all. A part of the recovery will be all about separating the past and present in your mind and not getting mixed up between both. It is true that once you were a helpless child but today, you have become a self-soothing, self-approving, self-caring, and assertive person.

Identify the triggers of your childhood, and if you see them in today's age as well, you need to figure out a way to deal with them. Avoidance is not going to help you in the long run. You can perhaps take the help of a therapist to deal with the triggers. Codependents usually form certain illusions about dependency that drive them throughout their life. For example, you might be feeling responsible for the problems faced by your loved ones. The most common reason for this is being raised by controlling parents. If you do not deal with these thinking patterns, they will lead to unhealthy suppression of anger.

Deal with Your Reckless Impulsivity

Confusing and overwhelming emotions develop the moment you start becoming too much dependent on someone else other than yourself. That internal state often leads to impulsive reactions, which can be dangerous and unhealthy. You might think of something as a good idea when you are in a good mood, but the moment you step back and look at the bigger picture, the same idea might start to seem bad. But you need to make yourself understand that ups and downs are simply a part of your life. Calm yourself down by taking deep breaths or thinking about something good.

When intense feelings start flooding you, it might feel permanent. You may think that you are never going to get rid of them. But this is not true. If you give yourself enough time, every bad phase is eventually going to pass. You simply need to wait it out rather than reacting impulsively because that is only going to make matters worse.

The irony is that when you try to make things be over by reacting recklessly, they increase even more. You can try journaling to express your feelings somewhere privately instead of hurling bad words at someone you might later regret. It is also important to love yourself and sympathize with your current state because things can get overwhelming at times.

Recognize Your Clinginess at the Right Time

You need to perform self-introspection from time to time because that is going to reveal a lot of things about yourself that need attention. If you see that you have developed an 'all or nothing' attitude towards people, then you need to do something about it at once. This is a sign of premature attachment. It leads to an unnecessary sense of possessiveness, which can be suffocating for the other person. If you have just started to meet someone new, prevent getting too attached to him or her because when the level of involvement doesn't match on both sides, there can be a lot of complications in relationships.

Reciprocation is necessary for all relationships. If you are into premature attachment with someone, then you might end up giving them way too importance in your life than they deserve. So, give the relationship some time before getting too attached.

Chapter 10:

Take Initiative Towards Recovery by Following These Steps

Now that you know the basics of what codependency is and how you can deal with it, this chapter will give you a step-by-step approach towards recovery. You simply have to follow the guidelines mentioned here, and you will undergo a complete transformation.

Step 1—Admitting Your Powerlessness

Everything in life cannot be controlled. For example, if you have an addiction, you are powerless to it. In order to overcome that feeling, you first have to accept your powerless nature. But codependents have the inherent tendency to try and control everything in their life. They do this not only with material things but also with people because their happiness relies upon them. The behavior and thinking of codependents are centered on other people and how they can influence them.

Some codependents try to control other people because they want to avoid abandonment or loss. But that idea of controlling someone is nothing but an illusion. You can never really do it. Instead, the entire feeling keeps you in denial. Your life starts becoming less and less manageable because you are spending all your time trying to control something that cannot be controlled at all. You stay in

106

eternal denial. So, the moment you see that all your efforts are going in vain, you have to understand that it is time for you to accept your powerlessness in that respect. The understanding of this step will become clearer with time. Acknowledging a problem is always the first step to everything, and the second step is seeing the fact of how trying to manage the unmanageable is wreaking havoc in your life.

It will feel humbling to accept that you are powerless over others. Practicing non-attachment is not an easy task, as we have discussed in length in Chapter 6. This is because your ego comes in the way, and it never likes to become defeated. Even if things are becoming frustrating, futile, or exhausting, changing yourself or the efforts to do so can bring about resentment and anxiety. But you need to tell yourself that being powerless has nothing to do with helplessness. Sometimes, dealing with problems becomes way easier with inactions. It gives you a sense of clarity. Also, you will get better control over your mind. In order to face powerlessness, you need to ask yourself what do you think makes you happy. You also need to judge whether you can control the aspects of your happiness and if not, do you feel powerless over them. You need to see within your souls and judge whether you have the inherent feeling to keep everyone around you in control. Lastly, you also have to keep a note of those feelings that are stopping you from letting go of other toxic things in your life.

Step 2—Seek Hope

Recovery is only possible when you understand that there is still hope and so you have to find that hope. It can be tempting to leave everything in the face of adversity and return back to your old self. But you have to resist that feeling and find relief in other things, maybe your passions. This is step is more about getting assurance that this is not the end of the world, and there are lots of things left to do. You can spend some time each day to meditate because it will calm your mind and help you concentrate.

Step 3—Learn to Let Go

You should not let your ego control every action in your life. But in the case of codependents, ego definitely plays a central position. And so, you have to understand that you do not always have the outcomes in your hand. Thus, you have to learn to let go of certain things in life. There will be daily frustrations that can trigger the old you, but you have to stop trying to control everything as sometimes, you literally cannot do anything. Surrendering yourself, or the idea of it can be daunting to codependents because they come from a place of neglect and abuse.

But, on the other hand, trust is not built in a day. It is a process, and in order to move towards it, you have to learn to let go. Reality is more often than not painful. Even if everything is going well, there will be moments when you will think that something is missing, but that is okay. Your life is not meant to be perfect. You need to accept everything realistically because only then can you live effectively. But letting go doesn't mean you should not make goals. It simply means that you should not try to control the outcomes.

Step 4—Assess Yourself

Codependents are always so focused on others and their well-being that they never examine themselves. Their own feelings, behaviors, and thoughts go unexamined. But all of this leads to unhappiness because they are too preoccupied with others. They gradually become blind to the fact that their own behavior is self-destructive and may even be the cause of their unhappy state. They keep blaming others for their current predicament and remain in denial about facing the truth. But this step will teach you all about self-awareness, and you have to examine your thought patterns to find any dysfunctional nature.

But you should not use this step to shame or blame yourself. This step is purely meant for self-discovery and not self-loathing. You need to list all the things that you love and also all the things that you resent. You should also consider whether you are selfish, manipulative, or bitter. You might be tempted to justify your actions, but you have to resist such feelings. You need to pay careful attention to your emotions and write everything down. You also need to mention all those people whom you have hurt in the process.

Step 5—Share Your Shame

This is a crucial step because internalizing your shame will not benefit you in any way. When you bring forth the innermost feelings of your heart, you will feel lighter, and the shame will not accumulate inside of you. Thus, this step is about making yourself a bit vulnerable. You need to acknowledge the fact that you, too, have imperfections just like others on this planet. Shame can be paralyzing if not dealt with appropriately. It leads to depression and self-loathing. But the path to recovery starts with sharing your shame and showing empathy for yourself.

In the previous step, I had asked you to list the feelings and thoughts you have about yourself, but now it is time to choose a nonjudgmental person who will read through what you have written. That person can assist you in identifying the feelings that you have kept buried for a long time. But you also need to ensure that you have an open mind. This will open several potential opportunities for you, where you can learn more about yourself. Yes, it is true that what has happened in the past cannot be undone, but your perception of your past can definitely be changed. So, the moment you share your shame, you will start walking on the path of self-acceptance, which brings us to the next step.

Step 6—Accept Yourself

When you accept yourself, you will be gradually diminishing the ego from your soul. If you have come to this step of the process, then by now, you understand that awareness along will be of no help. You can accept yourself when you surrender your control over the different things in life. This step is more about a psychological transformation, and the process is not limited to just any single step. It will continue throughout the process. In the beginning, when you start to accept yourself, it can be frustrating. You will face difficulty to let go of your shortcomings and bad habits, even if your intentions are good. But with constant effort, you will get success.

You have to go through this phase with an attitude of self-compassion, and you should not be too hard on yourself. With time, as a codependent, you have always neglected the deeper problems of your own, but now is the time for confrontation. Becoming autonomous and assertive means that you have to develop some new skills as well, and this will take time. But when you reach the point of no return, that is exactly when you know you have to change at all costs, and you finally learn to accept yourself.

Step 7—Be Humble

You might be trying to change yourself for quite some time without any proper result, and you might even be ready to give up to despair. But then you will come to the point of humility, and you need to be ready to accept it with open arms. Humility does not signify you as a weak person. Instead, it is a sign of maturity. Till now, you have assessed yourself honestly and have understood that you have several shortcomings that are not within your reach of control. When you work with pride, you become authentic. You need to accept your frailty in order to know what it feels like to gain compassion.

Step 8—Keep a List of People You Have Hurt

With your ruthless behavior as a codependent, you surely must have hurt a lot of people in your life, and you shouldn't forget them. You need to make amends with these people. You cannot and should not justify what you did and nor should you state that you did it with good intention. First, you need to gather up the courage to make amends, and then you need to imagine making amends so that you get a little bit of practice. Don't simply jump into the situation without a plan. You should not forget to add your name to the list of people you have hurt because you definitely do not pay any interest to your opinion as a codependent. You do not have boundaries, and even if you do, they are dysfunctional and broken.

Step 9—Make Amends

Whenever you see an opportunity to make amends, grab it and do it. Codependents usually face trepidation when they are asked to make amends. But you need to take responsibility for everything that you have done till today and make necessary amends. It will also give you a clean slate to start with. Making amends might seem tough or daunting at first, but once you have done it, you will feel joyous and rewarding. Also, meet the other person face-to-face when you are making amends. Don't generalize while you are saying sorry. Be as specific as you can and don't beat around the bush.

This step also involves changing your bad behaviors while going forward in your relationship. You also have to take care of the fact that you don't end up hurting someone else when you are trying to relieve your own guilt. You should not be saying sorry with the expectation of being forgiven. You have to remember that you are making amends for your own personal satisfaction and not for others. In case you receive an abusive reaction from the person in front of you, you need to be ready to handle it. If you are making amends with someone very close to you, a strategy for not repeating your past mistakes should be present. If you keep repeating the things you are apologizing for, then the person loses his/her trust in you.

Making amends is not always about others. You need to make amends to yourself as well so that you can increase your self-esteem.

Step 10—Start With a Clean Slate Daily

Recovery is not about reaching a finishing point but about a continuing process. You should not be waiting forever to get things done. If something crops up in your mind, do it today; otherwise, it will keep accumulating in your heart. Also, the more time passes after an incident, the more the wound deepens, and the person in front of you receives a greater amount of sadness when you bring up old events. Your self-responsibility is enhanced with the power of making prompt amends. If something in your life feels wrong, you should take responsibility for it and make it right at once.

If you have gone through all the steps until now, then you will learn to prioritize everything, starting from your emotional serenity to your personal growth over the needs of others. Also, if you clean your slate daily, you will continue being honest with yourself. You can practice this at the end of the day before going to sleep. This will also prevent you from slipping back to your old habits and stick to your path. You can also check your journal for having a look at the things you are proud of and make it a habit to list three things every day that went well.

So, these were the 10 steps that you need to follow in order to walk on the path of recovery. If you want to overcome codependency, then knowing about these steps will never be enough. You have to put them to use too. You should be applying all the steps to every affair in your life. You cannot be deceitful in your business and honest with your partner. It will not help you in any way. You have to be honest in both. If resentment is always present at the back of your mind, then maintaining intimate relationships with someone can become quite difficult.

You also need to stay away from other people's problems. You can listen to others, but you should not get too much involved or wrapped up in their problems. You can become a master if you work on the practices daily without fail. If you keep at it for a long time, then transformation is assured sooner or later. Gradually, when you work each step daily, you will gain self-compassion, and this will take you a long way on the path of self-recovery. After you have completed all the steps of the process, you need to ask yourself—what changes have you seen in yourself. You will be able to define transformations in your way, and you will also learn to apply each of these steps in your daily life.

When you develop some new skill or quality, you will feel different, and you might even feel frightened. This is because new skills mean you are refraining from your old ways. But adopting these skills will take years of practice. Your manners when you were a codependent person were self-protective in nature, and so when you wanted to let go of them, you will face a lot of anxiety. You will also face the fear of abandonment, but no matter what, don't give in to the temptation of reverting back to your old self. But relapse will become even more likely if you do not indulge in self-care. So, nurture yourself and walk on the path of recovery for the future holds a lot of new possibilities and growth.

Chapter 11:

How to Stop Being Codependent and Make Relationships Work?

Healthy relationships exist only when you learn to overcome all dysfunctional habits. But in a codependent relationship, there are a lot of complex factors playing the role. If you are in a healthy relationship, then it will not keep you preoccupied in all instances. It should not be in the foreground. When in love, you cannot control who you fall in love with, but you can definitely ensure that your relationship is healthy by following some effective communication strategies. You need to nurture and care for your relationship if you want it to prosper. You also need to remember that love and hate go hand in hand. So, in case you feel intense hate towards your partner from time to time, it is not anything abnormal. There will be some disappointments in the relationship, but with a bit of effort, you can move past it.

So, if you want to make your relationship work, then read this chapter carefully.

Practice Individuation

Much of the work in building a healthy relationship is about individuation and building self-esteem. This means that you have to work upon your sense of self, and this is even more important for codependents because, in them, the sense of

116

self is completely or partially impaired since childhood. That is why codependents face difficulty in maintaining healthy intimate relationships.

So, the first step is to look at your childhood wounds. Are they still fresh, and do they still remind you of the agonizing times you had? If yes, then you have to work upon eliminating their effect and hold on to your present. When you heal those wounds, you will enhance your capacity to see your present in a better way. You will no longer see your present filtered through the light of the past but for the way it is. You will also be less triggered by things related to your childhood experiences. With individuation, you will learn to accept your parents, forgetting about past resentments.

In order to make a successful relationship, there has to be a union of two individuals, and this is nothing to do with blending. There are three separate entities in a relationship, and they are—I, you, and we. When there is a lack of individuation in a relationship, the whole focus falls on the 'you' and 'we,' and meanwhile, the 'I' is completely lost, overlooked, and forgotten. They always do things together and forget that they have some different interests too. When they ignore the differences, the codependent partner tries to control the other partner and will have the upper hand. But then there are others who feel threatened by closeness and thus prefer remaining isolated even from their partner.

No matter what the problem in your relationship is, everything ultimately revolved around the strength or fragility of your 'self.' It might sound weird, but it is true that you will be able to practice intimacy freely when you have a greater level of autonomy. There are two types of codependents. There are some who do not feel worthy of love and are thus the ones who push their partners away, and then there are others who are so threatened by the thought of abandonment that they always cling to their partners.

Sometimes there are power struggles too, and one partner is not sure whether they are forgoing too much independence for one person and whether that person is worth it or not. In such a situation, the relationship suffers, and it gets stuck because of mutual discontent.

But in a healthy relationship, couples believe in closeness but not in oneness. They enjoy their separate lives and at the same time, give enough priority to their relationship. So, the lesson is to work on developing your 'I' even if you are in a relationship because that will make the bond stronger.

What Are the Essential Qualities of Relationships That Last?

Your self-esteem plays a big role in ensuring a lasting relationship. You can overcome all the power struggles when you know that you do not fear being rejected or abandoned. A lasting relationship is one that creates a sense of safety and one where both partners accept each other's' differences openly. They solve the problems together, and they also make the decisions only after consulting each other on the matter. Even if they are lovers, they remain best friends first. They know how to communicate assertively.

They also behave realistically. Both partners share a common vision, and they not only spend quality time when they are together but also when they are apart. They cooperate on everything and give without wanting anything in return. They have compatible values and needs and continue pursuing their own goals and dreams, even if they are together. When they develop a high sense of self-esteem, they do not seek validation from anyone, and their sense of self is complete. In short, if you want to improve your relationship, you have to work on yourself first. Once you do that, you will become open-minded, and you will no longer be sensitive to what others think about you or criticism that others do. For easier conflict resolution, safety is a big aspect of every relationship. Both partners should be willing to listen to each other and respect each other. No one should be abusing either verbally or physically. When all these qualities are present, both partners feel safe to be around each other. With safety comes the chance to show your true self. You finally got your safe haven after facing neglect in your childhood, and this is how codependents prosper in intimate relationships—through mutual respect and maintaining a safe vibe. But at the same time, if the partners are not reliable and always fail to keep up with the promises, then the foundation of trust is eroded, and the partners know that they cannot count upon each other. Healthy and happy couples don't think unrealistically and have reasonable expectations too. They know that their initial phase of love and romance is only limited, and with time, the phase will take a different form. The relationship is not meant to complete their soul but only be a part of it. They understand that there is nothing called perfection and so they don't expect it as well. They love themselves for the way they are. They understand that every relationship has its own challenges and problems and that they simply have to deal with it. When love is present, even codependent couples are ready to talk through all problems.

Another important aspect of every long-lasting relationship is healthy communication. You need to share what you are truly feeling with your partner. You need to set proper boundaries, and if you want something from your partner, you need to ask for it. There should be no hidden expectations because your partner is not a psychic, and he/she will not magically come to know of your wishes. You need to make requests, but without any act of manipulation so that the other person does not feel threatened to give you the correct answer. There is nothing called a correct or wrong answer when it comes to relationships. Everyone has their own views.

Healthy communication does not mean that every day will be mushy and full of love. There should be enough room for resentment and anger, as well. And, there should be mutually agreeable ground rules too. There should be no physical attack or verbal abuse during those communications, and there should also be no blame game. If you see that the anger has started to escalate, then you both should agree on taking a timeout. But whatever strategy you use, make sure you don't stockpile all your anger.

Long-lasting couples are aware of each other's differences, and they respect it. They do not become angry in order to tolerate these differences, and neither do they try to change the other person. You should not expect someone to change for you because that is not what love means. And even if the person shows some change from their habitual traits, it will be soon enough when those natural habits return. And after all, it is up to you whether you want to accept the person for who they are or not.

Now that you know the inevitability of differences in relationships, you should also work on your problem-solving skills as a couple. There are some couples who leave the problems as they are because they fear conflict, and there are others who let only one person be the decider in every situation. But both these strategies will lead to anger and resentment at one point in time or the other. This will ultimately create walls between you two and lead to the development of hopelessness. Thus, these couples keep to themselves because they fear that whenever they come to confrontation, there will be conflict, and they will be distancing themselves even further. On the other hand, when couples can solve problems after consulting each other effectively, they do not give up halfway or do not blame each other for anything. They value each other's companionship and happiness over anything else, and so they are ready to make the necessary compromise too.

Happy couples know the importance of spending happy times together. It does not always have to be a lavish dinner or something like that because simply sitting in your bedroom and talking about life can be spending quality time. In case you both share a hobby, then finding commonality becomes way easier, but even if you don't, you will find something to do together if you really give your relationship that much priority. Alongside this, spending some time apart with your respective friends is also equally important. Your relationship should not be the only source of nourishment for you, and you should always be open to new experiences and new energy. Your romance will stay alive when you spend happy times with others, as well.

Cooperation is the key to put an end to power struggles. When you cooperate with each other, you take care of each other's needs. You do not indulge in a competition about meeting each other's needs. When couples have compatible needs, they are usually more satisfied than others. For example, if one partner has greater needs than the other, then there is always some room for disappointment. The cause is not always personal, but what is important is that both the partners have different priorities. The solution is to acknowledge this fact and accept your differences. You should try and be open to new experiences because it will bring a vibe of freshness.

You do not necessarily have to possess the same values, but what you need to have is somewhat compatible values so that they can sustain you in the long term. You don't have to have the same religious or political beliefs, but the values that you do possess should not be deal-breakers. Fidelity and honesty are the two most important values in a relationship to sustain long-term, and this should stay intact for both partners. You should also have the same sense of security; otherwise, you will face problems later on. Some people believe in going all in and spending all their money pursuing what they love, while there are others who believe in paying off their mortgage and building a more secure life for themselves. If the partners belong to these two separate categories, then making financial decisions can become a very difficult task in the future.

As already mentioned above, having a common vision or goal always acts as the glue to your relationship. It can be home after retirement or your business or anything. This also enables that all your commitment is directed towards something that you both love. This also generates a lot of excitement because you both are working on it together, and no one is forcing you to do so as you are doing it out of love.

Lastly, you need to learn to maintain friendships beyond your relationship. Codependents have the habit of staying in lockdown, but eventually, such a situation leads to suffocation and unhealthy ambiance. You should not be expecting someone to give you all the attention and meet all your needs without keeping some time for themselves or for others in their life. That is why encouraging the involvement of friends outside your relationship is crucial.

Understanding Intimacy and Autonomy

Everyone loves both intimacy and autonomy, both in fixed proportions. The worst-case among couples is when they have such weak boundaries that they can neither enjoy intimacy nor indulge in autonomy. They feel lonely and empty. They want to be with someone who makes them feel special and validate their presence, but the moment they are too close with someone, it creates problems of its own. Such relationships are very much unstable, and there is a lot of drama.

The next type of relationship is when couples are able to experience both intimacy and autonomy in a mutually exclusive manner. They can experience only one of them at a time. This is definitely a better condition than the previous type, but in this type, you will find one partner always staying dissatisfied and discontent that the other partner is not giving him/her enough attention. But when that person starts to show more intimacy, the other person might start feeling pressurized or claustrophobic.

Then there is the next type where one partner thinks that all the problems are associated with the other partner. But when they talk it over, things can be sorted out. Some couples are even able to acknowledge the fact that they were trying to project their feelings onto others. These couples are usually able to discuss their differences and how they long for intimacy and autonomy.

The next type of couple is aware of their differences, and they are even ready to be responsible for their actions. They are not afraid of their troubles or confrontation and can openly talk about their feelings. They do not blame each other or impose any expectations on each other. They do not involve themselves in pleasing their partners to the extent that they lose themselves. In these couples, there is a much greater level of choice and fluidity. They can be confident and strong at times, but at other times, they are fragile and incompetent. They are both self-reliant and dependent. But at times, they can temporarily become like the previously mentioned type of couple.

Then comes the last type of couple, which is very rare to find. Their levels of intimacy and autonomy are in equal proportions, and thus, there is harmony. They do not have any escalating tension or anger between them. They don't feel rejected or don't take matters personally. They have a properly maintained sense of self. When they are intimate with each other, they do not feel that they have lost their autonomy. Likewise, when they appreciate the autonomy of their individual selves, they feel more loved.

Conclusion

Thank you for making it through to the end of *Codependency No More: How to Cure Codependency, Start to Love Yourself and Fight for No More Codependent Relationship Ever*, let's hope it was informative and able to provide you with all of the tools you need to achieve your goals whatever they may be.

The next step is to implement the steps in real life. Codependency is something that you have acquired through your childhood experience, and it is something that has dominated you for a large part of your life, so overcoming it will definitely require a lot of patience and consistency. You cannot choose to give up. But you should not expect everything to be perfect either, as this will generate anxiety and pressure not to return to your old self. You need to understand that you are human, and it is okay to make mistakes. But you should not be dependent on someone and acknowledge the things you feel or do. Stop exaggerating your mistakes in your mind because it will only make things worse. No matter what you do, never neglect taking care of yourself because that itself forms a major part of recovery for codependents. Look back on your progress from time to time and give yourself some credit for the change that you have made. Forgive yourself for the things of the past and focus on building relationships that are healthy and positive.

Finally, if you found this book useful in any way, a review on Amazon is always appreciated!

Made in the USA
Middletown, DE
23 January 2021